The Best of

Staffordshire

Lindsey Porter

Published by

Landmark Publishing

The Oaks, Moor Farm Road West, Ashbourne, Derbyshire. DE6 1HD

Published in the UK by
Landmark Publishing Ltd,
The Oaks, Moor Farm Road West, Ashbourne, DE6 1HD
Tel: 01335 347349 website: landmarkpublishing.co.uk

ISBN 13: 978-1-84306-452-7

Print: Gutenberg Press Ltd, Malta
Cartography: Mark Titterton
Design: Mark Titterton

Front cover: Trentham Estate
Back cover, top: Great Haywood
Back cover, bottom-left: The Close, Lichfield Cathedral
Back cover, right: Dovedale from Stoney Low

Picture Credits

Courtesy of Alton Towers: p.7 & p.23 top-left; Trentham Estate: p.38; Gladstone Pottery Museum: p.39
Trentham Monkey Forest: p.46; Whitmore Hall: p.47 all; Courtesy of the Wedgwood Museum
Trust: p.50 all; Drayton Manor Park: p.79 top-left; Tutbury Castle: p.79 bottom; Weston Park: p.82;
RAF Museum, Cosford: p.86 bottom-left; Trentham Aerial Extreme: p.91 bottom;

Mark Titterton: p.7 bottom & p.18 bottom

All other photographs by Lindsey Porter

DISCLAIMER

While every care has been taken to ensure that the information in this book is as accurate as
possible at the time of publication, the publishers and author accept no responsibility for any
loss, injury or inconvenience sustained by anyone using this book.
Maps in this book are for location only. You are recommended to buy a road map.

Staffordshire

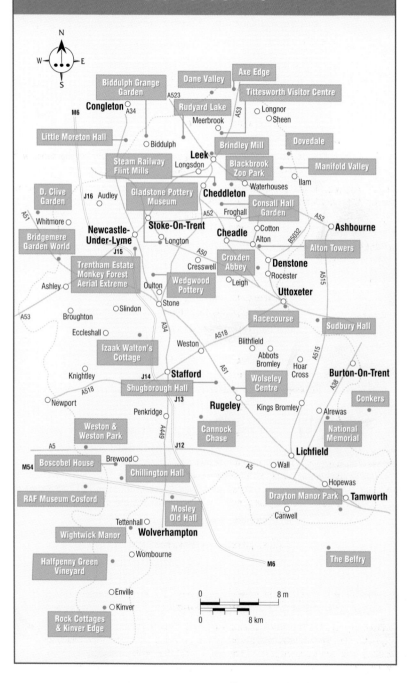

Contents

Top Attractions

Theme Parks or Attractions

Alton Towers, Alton pp.20, 25

Drayton Manor Park, nr Lichfield pp.78

Waterworld, Etruria, Stoke-on-Trent p.56

Conkers, Moira, nr Burton-on-Trent pp.80-1

RAF Museum, Cosford, nr Telford pp.85-7

Aeriel Extreme/Monkey Forest, Trentham p.56

Country Houses

Shugborough, nr Stafford p.64-5

Weston Park, Weston-under-Lizard p.85, 87

Whitmore Hall, Whitmore p.44

Wightwick Manor (N.T.), nr Wolverhampton p.84

Moseley Old Hall (N.T.), nr Wolverhampton p.85

Boscabel House (E.H.) p.86

Free to Visit

Royal Air Force Museum, Cosford, (except events) pp.85-7

County Council Country Parks p.52

Staffordshire Wildlife Trust Reserves p.8

Trentham Estate Retail Village p.48

Cannock Chase p.61

Ancient High House, Stafford p.60

Izaak Walton Cottage p.60

National Memorial Arboretum p.71

Lichfield Cathedra p.73

Gardens

Biddulph Grange (N.T.) pp.41, 44, 56

Consall Hall Landscape Garden p.51, 56

Dorothy Clive Garden p.45, 56

Trentham Estate pp.48-9

Whitmore Hall p.44, 56

Wightwick Manor pp.84, 85, 87

Staffordshire is fast becoming one of the most visited counties of middle England and before you query this, read on.

Top Tips Staffordshire

• **Alton Towers**: Nationally known theme park.

• **Cannock Chase**: Very large heathland/ AONB, lots of waymarked trails and lovely scenery.

• **Cheadle R.C. Church**: Probably the finest Gothic Revival Church anywhere (Pugin).

• **Dovedale & Manifold Valley**: Superb scenery in the Staffordshire Peak District.

• **Lichfield Cathedral**: Soak up the architecture/history in this superb House of God.

• **Shugborough Hall**: Combines the elegance of the house and the experience of seeing first hand bygone working environments.

• **Trentham Estate**: Fantastic recreated Italianate garden, shopping village and Monkey Forest.

• **Wedgwood Pottery Museum and Visitor Centre**: Factory tours, museum and shop.

• **Weston Park**: Treasure House and one of the finest Georgian parks in the country.

Two Gardens

Biddulph Grange Garden (NT): Acclaimed restored Victorian themed garden.

Consall Hall Landscape Garden: 70 acres of carefully designed gardens, lakes and woodland.

Top: Alton Towers; Middle: Cannock Chase; Bottom: Cheadle R.C. Church

The Staffordshire Wildlife Trust

The Trust acquired its first reserve in 1970 and now manages many of them. It has created concessionary paths over a good number for public access. They vary in terms of size and habit (see list below). The SWT welcome new members. Their headquarters are at the purpose built Wolseley Centre, Wolseley Bridge, Stafford ST17 0WT. (☎ 01889 880100)

A Nature Reserve Guide is available detailing each of the reserves where visitors are welcome. They extend from the 300 acre wetland reserve in the flood plain of the River Sow near Stafford at the Doxey Marshes, to a 2.8 acre site near Penkridge. From the flood plain there are other large sites in the Staffordshire Moorlands preserving moorland and heathland habitats.

All of the reserves are of course special and nature lovers will welcome the opportunity to visit some of the best habitats which the county has to offer.

Staffordshire Wildlife Trust Nature Reserves with concessionary public access:

Site	Size	Description
Allimore Green Common, Haughton	6.7ac	Lowland wet grassland
Bateswood nr Madeley Heath	61ac	Grassland and pools
Bickwood Meadows nr Penkridge	2.8ac	Wet meadows
Black Brook N of Ramshaw Rocks, nr Leek	298ac	Moorland and plantation
Black Firs and Cranberry Bog, nr Betley	15ac	Peatland of International importance
Black Heath and Casey Bank	100ac	Former limestone quarry
Brown End Quarry, Waterhouse	-	Former limestone quarry
Burnt Wood, loggerheads	30ac	Ancient oak woodland
Castern Wood, Wetton	51ac	Wood, scrub and grassland
Colwich Brickwork, Little Haywood	10ac	Wood, scrub and grassland
Cotton Dell, nr Oakamoor	160ac	Wood and grassland
Croxall Lakes nr Nat. Mem. Arboretum	104ac	Wetland
Doxey Marshes, nr Stafford	300ac	Wetland
George's Hayes, Cannock Chase	48ac	Woodland
Harston Wood, Froghall	67ac	Woodland
Hemheath Woods, nr Trentham	100ac	Woodland
Jackson's Coppice & Marsh, Bishop's Offley	20ac	Wetlands 'The Everglades of Staffordshire'
Loynton Moss nr Eccleshall	135ac	Woodland and wetland
Oakwood Pasture, nr Barton-under-Needwood	23ac	Woodland pasture
Parrot's Drumble, Talke Pits	30ac	Woodland
Pasturefields, Saltmarsh	19ac	Access by permit only – our last national inland salt marsh
Rod Wood, Cheddleton	40ac	Unimproved meadows, unimproved grassland
Side Farm Meadows, Cotton	10ac	Unimproved meadows, unimproved grassland
Thorswood, Stanton	150ac	Grassland/upland heath
Weag's Barn	45ac	Grassland/woodland

For a start, I acknowledge it will be unlikely to catch up with Derbyshire, for the Peak District National Park is the second most visited park in the world, Fujiama in Japan being the first (with c. 25 million visitors a year). However, half of one of the most visited destinations – Dovedale – is in Staffordshire and the whole of the lovely adjacent Manifold Valley and its tributary the Hamps are within the county. To the north-west, half of the upper reaches of the River Dane is in Staffordshire too.

Some of the county authority's border road signs call it the 'Creative County', but is it? As a Staffordshire lad, I thought the bottom of the county was lost within the urban depression still referred to as the Black Country, but I was wrong. Wolverhampton and Dudley left over forty years ago. Many of the big names in the Pottery Industry of Stoke-on-Trent now manufacture in the Far East, although a lot of Potteries-folk would seem to query the quality.

English Electric and many other big names have gone from Stafford, not forgetting the almost complete decline of textile manufacturing in Leek. However, the county was also creative in a cultural sense. Tamworth Castle, Lichfield Cathedral and Croxden Abbey remind us of the medieval achievements. Pevsner left Staffordshire to the last in his series 'Buildings of England'. He had good reason. Some of its secular architecture is (or was) the finest in the country. Five architects in the Gothic Revival style did their best ecclesiastical work in Staffordshire. Pugin's church at Cheadle is acknowledged as the finest of the style in the world. He also claimed that 'for picturesque grounds and garden furnishings, few houses in England can compete with Shugborough'.

If we no longer have the industry, we do have most of its cultural achievements. Barry's Trentham Hall has mostly gone but St Modwen Properties have refurbished his Italianate garden and added another 10 acres to it with plans to restore what remains of the house; Alton Towers is just a shell, but still an important one. It may yet see restoration into a profit-earning asset following St Modwen's pioneering example at Trentham. In the north of the county, the National Trust have done remarkably well with their restoration work at Biddulph Grange Garden and William Podmore's incredible achievement at Consall Hall's 70-acre Landscape Garden is beginning to receive the attention and praise it deserves.

Following on from Trentham Estate's rise like a phoenix from its slumbering state, is the £10-million new Wedgwood Museum at nearby Barlaston, exhibiting 6,500 to 7,500 items of its wares.

More country houses are beginning to open their doors, with Whitmore joining Sandon, Chillington, Weston Park and Casterne – albeit for limited periods only – and at Sandon, only for groups. Wedgwood Museum is not the only new museum, with the Etruria Industrial Museum at the junction of the Trent & Mersey and Caldon Canals now well established. Equally well established is the Potteries Museum, with the finest china collection in the world and the Gladstone Museum in Longton, preserving a 19th century pottery with a 'hands on' 21st century experience.

(continued on p.12)

Staffordshire Oatcakes

Staffordshire has a very distinctive oatcake. It is nothing like a cake, but is made from oatmeal. It is thin, about 8 – 9 inches in diameter and a little rubbery, the more so if not eaten while fresh. The oatmeal is mixed as below and cooking it could not be easier. It is put under the grill with a layer of cheese, onions and apple or whatever else takes your fancy and left until the topping is cooked.

Removed from the grill, it is then rolled up before serving. Oats were a staple diet in poor communities and also in poor agricultural areas, such as the Staffordshire Moorlands. Research by your author of The Hartington and Crowdecote Mills on the River Dove has shown that in the 18th century, the Miller spent most of his time grinding oats (as well as producing malt for beer making).

Leek has an oatcake shop, in Brook Street and their oatcakes are made on the premises, but they are closed after lunchtime. The oatcakes are also available at grocers and some butchers.

Oatcake Mixture

½ lb fine oatmeal; 6oz strong plain flour;
2oz Hovis wholemeal flour; 1oz yeast (2 x 7gm dried);
1 pint milk; 1 pint warm water; Salt;
Skimmed milk or plain white flour can be used.

Preparation:

Cream yeast in a little warm water and milk.
Mix oatmeal, flour, milk and water together.
Add creamed yeast, add salt to taste.
Leave in a warm place for 30 minutes or so.
If mixture is too thick add small amount of water.
Makes approximately 24 – 28 oatcakes.

Nigel Burnett's family recipe from Ipstones

The oatcakes in the photograph are on an original oatcake spatula

Opposite page top-left: Bratch Locks Wombourne; Top-right: Gladstone Pottery Museum; Bottom-left Trentham Estate Garden and Bottom-right: Ilam Rock, Dovedale

What a pity Leek has not capitalised on the work of William Morris in the development of modern vegetable dyes; the Leek Embroidery School and the Arts & Crafts architecture so prevalent there, let alone one of those top five Gothic Revival churches mentioned above.

If your visit is more for fun than culture, Alton Towers and Drayton Manor Park attract impressive numbers of visitors seeking the thrill of bare-knuckle rides and the like. For heart-warming rather than heart-stopping activity, the county has captivating countryside waiting for you to put your boots on or get on your bike in some of the best scenery on offer away from the mountains and coastal paths, especially in the Staffordshire Moorlands and on Cannock Chase.

If less grand from a scenic point of view, the burgeoning National Forest has much to offer around its 'Conkers' Visitor Centre at Moira. Although just over the county border, much of the Forest area is within Staffordshire.

Additionally, we now have an excellent number of local authority country parks and nature reserves (run by the Staffordshire Wildlife Trust), with lots of trails and paths, let alone long distance walking trails.

The growth of what might have been secondary visitor areas such as the National Forest, Cannock Chase and the Churnet Valley, all with a former industrial base shows how much of the county has responded to the needs of visitors. It also shows how increasing visitor numbers indicate people's interest in what the county has to offer and an appreciation of the hard work of local authorities, businesses and many individuals. Together they have heightened the quality of what Staffordshire can offer the fun-loving and the discerning visitor alike.

So I suppose we are the creative county from the point of cultural achievement and in creating quality attractions for you, the visitor. Now we need to create a better strap-line on some of the road signs on our county's boundary. Staffordshire deserves it.

The text herein shows a bias in length towards the Staffordshire Peak District. This is deliberate and reflects the huge visitor numbers to this area compared to other parts of the county. Dovedale alone receives over one million visitors a year and copes remarkably well with it.

Lindsey Porter

Treasures of the Gothic Revival

Staffordshire has some lovely churches, let alone its magnificent Cathedral at Litchfield. In north Staffordshire alone, there is the largely wooden church at Rushton (in a field between the Parishes of Rushton James and Rushton Spencer) as well as the nearby ancient churches of Horton, Leek and Cheddleton. Ilam Church retains some Saxon architecture, one of only two (Tamworth being the other) to do so in the county.

Until Father Michael Fisher of St Chads, Stafford published his *Vision of Splendour* (now available in a revised 2nd edition as *Staffordshire and the Gothic Revival*, it was little realised that the county has the best ecclesiastical work of five architects in this style. In the six midland counties of Cheshire, Derbyshire, Shropshire, Warwickshire, Worcestershire and Staffordshire there are 137 Gothic Revival Churches and nearly 40% of these (52) are in Staffordshire. The five architects (and their Staffordshire Churches) are Bodley (3), Pugin (16), Scott (16), Shaw (3) and Street (14). Their best church is:

G. F. Bodley	Holy Angels, Hoar Cross
A. W. N. Pugin	St Giles, Cheadle (RC Church)
G. G. Scott	St Mary's, Stafford
R. N. Shaw	All Saints, Leek
G. E. Street	All Saints, Denstone

It is generally recognised that Cheadle is the best of these and probably the best Gothic Revival Church anywhere. If you think you do not know the style, think no further than the Palace of Westminster.

Of the secular buildings, Alton Towers was one of the finest dwellings in the style anywhere. Today it is a huge shell, but an important one, situated in the midst of the theme park. It was the house of the Earl of Shrewsbury, the 16th Earl, who also built Cheadle RC Church with A. W. N. Pugin.

Elsewhere, Ilam Hall and Butterton Hall (south west of Newcastle –under-Lyme) have both been demolished, although a little remains at Ilam as the Youth Hostel. Just over the county boundary, below Ashbourne, Cottingham built Snelston Hall in the same style, but that too was demolished in the early 1950s.

Of survivors, most are private, but one which may be seen easily and may well amuse is Speedwell Castle in Brewood, south west of Penkridge. Built with the proceeds of a bet on the Duke of Bolton's horse, Speedwell, it dates from 1850 and is in the Market Place.

The Upper Churnet and Dane Valleys

The far north east part of the county is an area of open and often treeless moorland dissected by river systems with attractive valleys of small fields and some woodland. Flowing off the high moors, these valleys offer good walking and extensive views. There is much to see.

The Axe Edge moors afford good views over quite a large area. From the lay-by just south of the Mermaid Inn on **Morridge** one can, for instance, see to the Welsh Hills and the Wrekin in Shropshire on a clear day. Beyond the latter and 65 miles away, the Breiddens may be seen, just to the right and beyond The Wrekin. The more immediate view down to the Roaches and Ramshaw Rocks is perhaps more spectacular. If your route takes you up the Leek-Buxton road past Ramshaw Rocks, drive slowly looking for the rock, which obviously resembles a face. Known as the Winking Eye rock, it does just that as you drive past it.

The infant waters of the R Churnet flow into **Tittesworth Reservoir**, which can be seen shimmering on a summer's day below the Roaches. There is a good Visitor's Centre where the road to Meerbrook crosses the water. Great for the kids, it also has a shop, café and exhibitions as well as plenty of recreational land surrounding the buildings.

The Churnet Valley

The water of the valley spawned textile industries, which developed to take advantage of its power and purity. **Leek** developed as a textile town producing

Below: The Caldon Canal, Consall Forge

15

silk. Dyestuffs were produced in great quantities, particularly in the 19th century when it was found that the water could be used to produce the raven-black dyes for which the town became so famous and which were so popular with the Victorians. Old textile mills mingle with silk workers' houses, but none are open to the public.

A walk around Leek's main streets reveals the Victorian influence particularly under the design of the Sugdens, a local firm of architects. They designed many buildings in the town in the Arts and Crafts style. In the Market Place is a Butter Cross, dating from 1671. The town's corn mill in Mill Street has been preserved and is worth a visit. It is claimed by enthusiasts to have been built by James Brindley, who had his workshop nearby. The waterwheel and all its machinery are intact and in working condition and the second floor has been developed as a museum to Brindley. Although better known as a canal engineer, his early career was as a millwright.

Dieulacresse Abbey at Leek has been completely destroyed except for a small part of a pillar, but of comparable age is the town's parish church, which is well worth a visit. The church of St Edward the Confessor at Leek was founded in 1042. It has a beautiful pair of 13th-century rose windows and some ancient crosses in the churchyard. Despite alterations over nearly a thousand years, much of interest remains of the old church. A guide book is on sale in the vestry.

Two churches of similar age to Leek are at Cheddleton and Horton, situated about 4 miles (6km) south and west of Leek respectively. Further north Rushton church, situated in the fields halfway between Rushton James and Rushton Spencer so as to serve both villages, is well worth a visit, as is the Forest Chapel north of Wildboarclough which was erected in 1673 and rebuilt in 1834. Here the annual rush laying ceremony in August can be observed (and yes it is a little north of the county boundary, but this unusual custom deserves a mention!).

Visitors are welcome at the **RSPB Coombes Valley Nature Reserve**, which protects woodland and pasture in the Coombes Valley, a tributary of the Churnet, between Cheddleton and Ipstones near to Leek. This can be approached from the A52 Leek to Ashbourne road and a few miles further along this road is the **Blackbrook Zoological Park**. A large and varied collection of rare and endangered species are housed here with birds a particular speciality. The zoo is involved in a number of breeding programmes helping to save rare species from extinction.

At **Cheddleton** on the A520 south of Leek is the preserved **Cheddleton flint mill**. The picturesque site is adjacent to the Caldon Canal and a preserved narrow boat is moored here. Flint stones were calcined in kilns and ground to powder, then used in the Potteries to make bone china, hence its local importance. With two working waterwheels, the mill has become an important tourist attraction where the whole process is demonstrated.

At Cheddleton, the old railway station about a mile downstream from the mill can be visited. It has a collection of steam locomotives and rolling stock and a museum devoted to the North Staffordshire Railway. From the station the **Churnet Valley Railway** runs steam and diesel services over a 10.5 mile (17km) stretch of restored track through the valley to Froghall. A new station and visitor centre has been built at Froghall. Trains run most weekends and some weekdays in high season. Passengers can alight at Consall or Froghall and walk back to Cheddleton along the Caldon Canal or simply enjoy a picnic and catch a later service back.

The main appeal of the Churnet lies below Cheddleton, where the valley bottom can be followed along the canal towpath to Froghall. If you are particularly interested in canals and their architecture, take your car to Denford, just off the Leek to Hanley road (A53) at Longsdon. Walk westwards past the canal-side pub (the Hollybush) under the aqueduct, which carries the Leek arm of the canal, to **Hazelhurst locks**. There is a canal keeper's cottage, a fine cast-iron footbridge and much to interest the photographer.

Parking is difficult in Denford and an alternative way to explore that part of the canal and to enjoy some lovely countryside is to park at **Deep Hayes Country Park,** which is close by. It is then a short walk to The Hollybush and the locks.

The Cheddleton to Froghall section really starts at Basford Bridge near the railway station. The valley is well wooded and the leafy glades provide a marvellous backcloth for the canal. Consall Forge is a small hamlet on the canal. Steep steps descend from each side of the valley to reach it, giving a more direct access than

along the canal towpath.

On Sundays a canal boat with crew in period costume operates in summer from **Froghall Wharf,** offering a cruise with lunch or afternoon tea. Book beforehand if possible as it is very popular. Although the valley between Froghall and **Oakamoor** is denied even to the rambler, the latter village is worth investigation. It has two old pubs and a huge picnic site on the foundations of an old copper works, demolished in 1963. Here Messrs Thomas Bolton & Sons manufactured the copper wire core for the first transatlantic cable in 1856. Other than a few date stones, nothing now remains of the works except for a very large mill pool, the retained water cascading down a stepped weir before disappearing under the road bridge.

The section of valley between Oakamoor and Alton offers a choice of routes. The road via **Farley** leaves the valley, affording views of the latter and the Weaver Hills. It goes through Farley village with its attractive cottages and beautiful hall. Beyond Farley, the views are towards Alton Towers, its turrets soaring above the trees. The more direct route to Alton keeps to the valley bottom. On reaching the former Pink Lodge, now a café and restaurant, one can walk westwards up **Dimmingsdale** to the former mill and its attractive pools beyond. The café, now known as **The Rambler's Retreat Coffee House,** (☎ 01538 702730) is very popular in what used to be quite a quiet, secluded area. There is a large car park for visitors to Dimmingsdale, adjacent to the café.

Alton village once enjoyed the patronage of the Earls of Shrewsbury who

Brindley Mill, Leek

St. Edward Street, Leek

Above left: Cheddleton Flint Mill Right: Cheddleton Station, on the steam railway

Hazelhurst Locks and the Caldon Canal (left) and Leek arm (right), Denford

owned almost everything in the area. Look out for the village lock-up and the castle. The valley bottom at Alton has much to offer. The view up to the castle, perched high on the rocks above, looks like a Rhineland replica. The old railway station, has been restored by the Landmark Trust and is now available to rent by the week, while opposite is an old watermill. Look out for the lodge to the Towers, designed by Pugin as was the castle across the valley.

If you are standing looking at the station from above the old railway line, look over to your left. The outline of the old millpond can be seen. It was narrowed to make way for the Froghall – Uttoxeter branch of the Caldon Canal, but the latter was later filled in and used as the trackbed of the railway. Some long stretches of the canal exist between Alton and Denstone. The old railway line between Oakamoor and Denstone is now a cycle track Greenway.

Pervading over the immediate area is the distant rumble of the rides of **Alton Towers**, now the nation's leading amusement park. If it's fun and frights which drive you on, look no further. The house here remains as a shell, but you can wander around much of it at roof top height. It was arguably the finest Gothic Revival house in the country. There are two hotels on site if you wish to stay at the park overnight.

The Dane Valley

The Dane Valley, with its tributary the Clough Brook, rivals the Churnet and Dove Valleys as a major beauty spot in the west of the Peak District. Rising on Whetstone Edge, close to the Cat and Fiddle Inn, its deeply-cut valley confines the infant waters of the river. Using old packhorse routes as paths it is possible to walk down much of the valley. The old bridge at **Three Shires Head** should not be missed. Have a look underneath it to see that the bridge has been widened at some time, either for increased horse traffic or for the passage of carts.

A couple of miles downstream from the bridge is Gradbach, a scattered community with no village as such. It is easily approached off the A53 – the Leek to Buxton road – through Flash, which at 1,525ft (469m) is the highest village in England. This is a harsh village of weather worn cottages, huddled together on the side of Oliver Hill. Descending down to the Dane, the scenery is more interesting and the climate more tolerant.

Gradbach is worth taking time to explore. Lacking a village centre, it is best to park at the car park on the lane to the youth hostel and by the side of the river. Look out for the old Methodist Chapel, built in 1849, and the adjacent cottage by the bridge over the river Dane, before walking downstream towards Gradbach Mill and Back Forest. The mill is easy to find, simply take the road to Flash from the bridge and turn first right down the side of a small brook. This is however a narrow road; once the car park is reached it is better to park there and walk.

Gradbach Mill, now owned by the Youth Hostels Association, used to be a silk mill with a large waterwheel fed by water from the Dane. It was rebuilt in 1758 following a fire, and closed down as a silk mill about 100 years later. Its large waterwheel was scrapped in the 1950s.

Below the mill lies **Lud Church** and Back Forest, a large wood. Lud Church (SJ987657) is in the wood and is a huge cleft (landslip) worth seeking out. On reaching the end of the cleft, paths lead on to Danebridge, where there is a pub for lunch and a path back up the river to Gradbach, starting by the bridge. It is one of the best paths in the county.

Inns in the Clouds

Axe Edge and nearby Morridge have four of the highest inns in the country. *The Cat and Fiddle* is the second highest in the country (after Tan Hill). A little lower are *The New Inn*, Flash and *The Traveller's Rest* at Flash Bar. *The Mermaid Inn* on Morridge is not much lower.

Just above Danebridge, which straddles the county boundary running down the middle of the River Dane, the waters of the Clough Brook, coming down from Wilboarclough (also worth exploring) and the Dane unite to form a good sized river. It flows beneath the broad arch after which the village takes its name. Like many neighbouring communities, **Danebridge** consists of a few loosely grouped cottages. It also has an interesting old pub, the Ship Inn,

which until recently had some relics of Bonnie Prince Charlie's 1745 uprising, including a flintlock of a Scottish soldier and part of a newspaper he was carrying. The name Ship Inn is said to be a reminder of the *S S Swithamley* [sic], although the present inn sign is of the *Nimrod*, which took Shackleton, and Sir Phillip Brocklehurst of nearby Swythamley Hall, to the Antarctic.

The broad fields below Danebridge, broken by areas of woodland and views of Bosley Cloud, make a pleasant walk to **Gig Hall Bridge**, where the feeder channel to Rudyard Lake reservoir starts. Above the valley on the Cheshire side is Wincle Grange Farm where the monks of old had a sheep and cattle farm. Further north, connected by a track to the grange, is Cleulow Cross, now hidden by the trees that surround it. It was probably a waymark cross on the route to the coast from Dieulacresse Abbey at Leek, which had important holdings of sheep and is known to have exported wool to Italy.

From Gig Hall Bridge, the feeder supply winds down the valley to Rushton. It has a path at the side, much in the nature of a towpath, which provides a pleasant walk. Below the village lies Rudyard Lake, built in 1797 by John Rennie as a water supply to the Trent and Mersey Canal and today a popular resort for visitors. The **Rudyard Lake Steam Railway** runs from here. A new visitor centre has been built near the dam, which offers something for everyone with facilities for fishing, boating, picnics, birdwatching and walking. In case you have been wondering, Rudyard Kipling was named after the lake; his parents met here.

Top-left: Consall Hall Landscape Garden; top-right: Consall Forge;
middle-right: Froghall Wharf; bottom: Rudyard Lake steam railway

Top-left: The Log Flume at Alton Towers; top-right: Alton Towers Gardens;
bottom-left: The Loaf and Cheese Rock, Ramshaw Rocks, near Leek; bottom-right: Gradbach

Places to Visit

Tittesworth Reservoir

Meerbrook, 4 miles (6.5km) north of Leek ST13 8SW

☎ 01538 300400

www.st.water.co.uk

Open all year except Christmas Day. Walks around the reservoir, play area, visitor centre, café, scented garden and parking for Roaches' park and ride service. Free entry.

Leek

Brindley Water Mill

Mill Street

☎ 01538 483741

Open: Easter-Sep, weekends and Bank Holiday Mondays, 2-5pm; late July and Aug, also Mon, Tue and Wed 2-5pm. Operational cornmill. Museum of the life and times of James Brindley, engineer 1716-72.

Coombes Valley Nature Reserve

Six Oaks Farm, Nr Apesford, ST13 7EU Off A523 Ashbourne to Leek road

☎ 01538 384017

www.rspb.org.uk

Open: Daily 9am-9pm (or dusk). Free entry. Visitor centre open daily 9am-5pm.

Blackbrook Zoological Park

Winkhill, off A523 south of Leek ST13 7QR

☎ 01538 308293

www.blackbrookzoo.co.uk

Open: 10.30am-5.30pm, summer (dusk in winter).

Collection of birds and animals, many endangered species. Tea room, shop.

Churnet Valley

Cheddleton Flint Mill

Cheadle Rd, Cheddleton, Leek ST13 7HL

☎ 01782 502907

www.ex.ac.uk/~akoutram/cheddleton-mill

Open: Wed, Sat and Sun 1pm-4.30pm, most weekends 10.30am-5pm, closed Christmas and New Year.

Watermill which tells the story of the preparation of materials for the pottery industry. Free entry.

Churnet Valley Railway

Cheddleton, Leek, Staffordshire 3 miles (5km) from Leek, off A520 to Stone

☎ 01538 360522 Sundays;

www.churnetvalleyrailway.co.uk

Open: Weekends, Bank Holiday Mondays and some weekdays in high season.

Ornate Victorian station building housing café, souvenir shop and small relics museum. Also signal box and locomotive display hall. Picnic area. Steam rides on most open days. Regular special events.

Foxfield Steam Railway

Blythe Bridge ST11 9EA

☎ 01782 396210

www.foxfieldrailway.co.uk

Open: Times vary ring for details.

Museum, shop, buffet and bar and 3 mile (5 km) steam trips on colliery line to Dilhorne Park Station.

Deep Hayes Country Park

2 miles (3.2km) west of Leek, off A53

☎ 01785 277264

www.staffordshire.gov.uk

Mix of woods, meadows and pools with self-guided walks and nature trails. Visitor centre, picnic area, small shop.

Consall Nature Park

Consall

☎ 01543 871773

Open: all year, small shop open Apr–Sep.

Walks, fishing and picnic facilities; visitor centre with displays on nature conservation.

Froghall Wharf

A52 Ashbourne to Stoke road

Picnic area and restored limekilns

Canal Boat Trips, see below

Froghall Wharf Passenger Boat Service

ST10 2HJ

☎ 01538 266486

Open: end of May to early Sep

Crew in period costume offer canal trips with Sunday lunch or Sunday afternoon tea. Plus Thursday mornings at 10.30am pre-booking recommended; trips and group charter throughout the week.

Froghall Station

Churnet Valley Railway Station

☎ 01543 871773 for information.

Rudyard

Rudyard Lake

ST13 8XB 3 miles (5km) north of Leek, A523

Lake Ranger ☎ 01538 306280

www.rudyardlake.com

Shop/café open Easter–end-Sep otherwise weekends, boat launch slipway, bird watching, angling, walking, cycling.

Rudyard Lake Steam Railway

3 miles (5km) north of Leek, A523 ST13 8PF

☎ 01538 306704 www.rlsr.org

Open: every Sun and Bank Holiday from late Feb–Oct plus Sat Easter–end-Sept.

Runs from former B.R. station to the lake.

Alton Towers

Alton

☎ 0870 444 4455

www.altontowers.com

Open: Easter (or 1st week in April)–1st week in Nov, 9.30-5.30pm.

Dovedale & the Manifold Valley

Many people regard Dovedale as a Derbyshire dale. Actually, half of it is in Staffordshire and with the Manifold Valley, plus its tributary, the River Hamps, Staffordshire can claim some of the most glorious scenery in the country outside the Lake District.

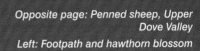

The infant Dove and Manifold both rise close to the Travellers Rest Inn at Flash Bar some 7.5 miles (12km) up the Buxton road out of Leek. The River Dove forms the county boundary between Derbyshire and Staffordshire. Its source is found in a small well close to the road, marked with intertwined initials of CC and IW – Charles Cotton and Izaak Walton. The Manifold's source can also be seen from the road, just to the south of the inn. Starting in a shallow depression, it is deeply cut into the landscape before leaving the field in which it rises.

The upper reaches of both rivers are spectacular. Take the Hollinsclough road from the Traveller's Rest Inn. The road soon climbs Edge Top where one can pull off the road and view both valleys at the same time. At this point the Manifold has cut deeply into the gritstone formations but the more spectacular view is towards **Hollinsclough** and the hills beyond.

Here there is a succession of hills on the edge of the limestone plateau, which stretch down the Dove and the Manifold. Examples include Hollins Hill, Chrome Hill, Parkhouse Hill and High Wheeldon. These are the closest approximations to 'peaks' in the Peak District.

Beyond Hollinsclough, the character of the two valleys changes. The Dove flows through a deep limestone valley past Crowdecote, while the Manifold, still flowing across the softer overlying shales, occupies a very broad and shallow valley. This difference can easily be seen by taking the Longnor to Sheen road, running along the rounded bluff between the rivers that at one point are less than a mile apart.

Below Hartington and Hulme End, both rivers occupy gorge-like valleys cut deeply into the limestone. The broad valley of the **Manifold** suddenly ends at the huge limestone dome of Ecton Hill. Hereafter it is characterised by huge incised meanders (a geological term approximating to large loops in a river found in a deep gulley rather than a flat meadowland) until the two rivers unite. It is these meanders ('many folds') that give the river its name, and they create an ever-changing subject for the eye and camera. As a result the scenery is more varied than the Dove Valley until one reaches the Milldale to Thorpe Cloud section of the River Dove.

This is **Dovedale** – a majestic stretch of the valley now absorbing a million visitors a year. With its natural ash woods, numerous towers of natural stone and features such as Pickering Tor, The Twelve Apostles, Reynard's Arch and the Watchbox near Ilam Rock, it has much to commend it. Dovedale is protected by the National Trust and the dale forms the major part of the Trust's South Peak Estate. It is also a Site of Special Scientific Interest, Grade 1, because of its ancient ash wood.

Union of the rivers

Between Ilam and Thorpe the two rivers unite. The Manifold is by far the larger river but, as the Dove is the county boundary, the latter carries its name down-stream from here until it reaches the River Trent near Burton. One of the main tributaries of these two rivers is the Hamps which flows off Morridge near to Leek, in a very broad valley to Waterhouses where it too reaches the limestone and enters a deeply incised valley like the Manifold. It twists and turns with almost monotonous regularity until it joins the Manifold beneath the huge cliffs of Beeston Tor, which was purchased by the National Trust in 1976.

Famous people

Historical and literary associations with the area are numerous, particularly as a result of the popularity of Dovedale. Byron and Dr Johnson for example were visitors to the dale; Jean Jacques Rousseau knew it during his exile at nearby Wootton Hall; William Morris and other pre-Raphaelites, as well as Mark Twain, were visitors to Sir Thomas Wardle at Swainsley in the Manifold Valley.

Perhaps the greatest name associated with the Dove is that of Izaak Walton who used to stay with his close friend – who became his adopted son – Charles Cotton. Cotton owned the Beresford Hall estate through which flowed the Dove. Beresford Dale was one of the prettiest places on the whole of the river, although Dutch elm disease killed many trees and their removal has marred the dale. It was here that Cotton built a fishing house, dated 1674, which still survives.

The area was penetrated by the narrow gauge (30in (76cm)) railway that ran down the Hamps Valley and up the Manifold Valley from Waterhouses to Hulme End. This railway opened in 1904 and ran for 30 years. The old station waiting room (now the Manifold Valley Visitor Centre) still remains at Hulme End. It was an unusual railway, with locomotives modelled on those from a narrow gauge line in India. The station waiting room contains a layout of the station with a model train.

The River Dove Described

The **River Dove** rises on Axe Edge, close to the Leek to Buxton Road. Although it is only a small stream, it has a pronounced valley within half a mile (800m) or so of the source. It flows below Brand Top, where the simple war memorial records the loss of five men from one family. There are a lot of packhorse routes in this area and footpaths now follow many of these old trails. Several cross the infant river with a single large slab of stone acting as a bridge. A substantial packhorse bridge survives at Washgate, 2 miles (3.2km) below the source. It has low walls to allow uninterrupted passage of the horses and their side panniers.

The Dove Valley is unusual in that it is possible to walk down the first 20 miles (32km) of its course, all the way to Ashbourne. You need to use the 1:25000 Ordnance Survey White Peak Map and do it in stages, perhaps as circular walks or with a car waiting ahead.

Below Glutton, the small river trickles along in a deep and fairly wide valley. The harder limestone rocks on the east side are higher than the softer gritstones on the west side. It is relatively quiet all the way down the valley to Hartington where the tourists flock daily. The walking is very pleasant too, through pasture and on farm tracks or quiet lanes. There is a pub – the Packhorse – at Crowdecote, where you can relax before continuing on towards Pilsbury and Hartington.

At **Pilsbury**, there is a motte and bailey castle on the Derbyshire bank with an interpretation board, explaining a little about this Norman fortification. Pilsbury was on an important saltway that crossed the Peak from Cheshire via the Roaches, Mermaid Inn and Brund (where it divided, one route going to Hartington and Wirksworth, the other via Pilsbury to Monyash and on to the eastern side of the Peak).

Hartington is situated on the Derbyshire side of the river, where Hartington Dale joins the Dove. There is a pottery producing terracotta ware and the Hart in the Country store. Hartington also benefits from various tea rooms, and the Charles Cotton Hotel (recently refurbished). The village is a good starting point for walks in the area, particularly into Dovedale.

Below Hartington, the valley becomes a gorge, the meadows ending abruptly at **Beresford Dale**. Charles Cotton lived in Beresford Hall, but it had become a ruin by 1850 and has now gone completely. The dale used to be quite dark from the leaf cover, but Dutch elm disease completely changed the dale's character. Look out for the **Prospect Tower** rebuilt in 1905-6 with stone from the remains of the hall, and also for the **fishing temple**. The latter is situated on a bend in the river and dates from 1674.

The valley is deeper in the next dale,

Wolfscote Dale, and the character stays like this all the way to beyond Milldale, where it becomes more wooded. **Milldale** is a popular place, despite being very small. It has a small shop that sells basic refreshments; a car park and toilets. The valley path uses the road between Lode Mill and Milldale. However a path runs along the top of the valley from Milldale to the Lode Mill to the Alsop-en-le-Dale road with splendid views down into the dale. The National Trust rightly has resisted pressure to open the other side of the river to ramblers – it is the last piece of limestone pasture in the valley on the Derbyshire side to remain without a path. Here is a good case of conservation taking priority over visitors.

Below Milldale lies **Dovedale,** with its limestone tors and relict ash wood, now a Grade 1 Site of Special Scientific Interest. The valley is very popular, and a causeway built along the pathway seems to contain the pressure from over a million visitors each year. The area around the tall **Ilam Rock** is particularly scenic. There is a footbridge here and land on which to sit and absorb the beauty around you. There used to be a wooden tearoom at the west end of the footbridge but this has long gone. The bridge takes one over to the path in Hall Dale and affords an opportunity to watch the fish and wild ducks on the river. The freestanding tors in Dovedale are probably the tallest in the Peak District and Ilam Rock may be the highest in England.

Below Ilam Rock are **Pickering Tors**, the **Lion Head Rock**, **Tissington Spires** and **Lovers Leap** before one reaches the **Stepping Stones** and

*Top-left: Ilam school; top-right: Wetton Mill bridge, built 200 years ago;
bottom: Dovedale from Stoney Low with Biggin Dale on the right*

the end of the gorge. The valley then becomes much more shallow as it continues on to Coldwall Bridge – a huge and unused turnpike era road bridge, Mapleton and the Okeover estate.

The section between Beresford Dale and the Stepping Stones differs from the rest of the valley. The river is flowing across a gravelly limestone river bed, the water is crystal clear and the path tends to hug the river. It therefore creates more interest than walking through the middle of river meadows, which characterise the rest of the Dove and the Manifold/Hamps light railway trail.

At the Stepping Stones you can leave the Dove and climb up Lin Dale to reach **Thorpe** and the Peveril of the Peak Hotel, which is built at the side of the footpath. When most visitors came by train (or on foot) from Ashbourne, this was the main way to Dovedale. Beyond the Stepping Stones, the river joins the Manifold below the Izaak Walton Hotel. The dining room here looks out onto Dovedale and has one of the best views from any hotel dining room in the country.

The Hamps and Manifold Valleys Described

The River Hamps

West of Dovedale lie the Manifold Valley and the upper basin of the **River Hamps**. Paths across the area are recommended to ramblers and it is easy to organise a circular route. There are many paths in this valley all the way down to Winkhill on the A523, where the valley becomes flat and featureless before turning north and into the limestone. Spring is a good time of year for walking here. Marsh marigolds and lady's smock add a splash of colour to the lush vegetation as one strolls along in quiet and unspoilt surroundings. Downstream there is little of interest in Onecote village, but the small collection of houses in **Ford** 1.5 miles (2.4km) further downstream is often missed by visitors.

The River Hamps changes its character completely at **Waterhouses**, where it leaves the grit and shales and enters limestone country. The river often disappears underground for months on end in dry weather, but rises again at Ilam. The valley meanders between steep hillsides to **Beeston Tor**, where it meets the Manifold Valley.

The track bed of the old light railway runs up the valley from Waterhouses. Cyclists are now permitted on the track and there are cycle-hire facilities in the old station car park and at Brown End Farm in Waterhouses. It presents a marvellous way of exploring the Manifold

Hulme End

Valley as far as Hulme End. The best way to return is down the same track; there is as much of interest travelling back as one sees when travelling up the valley, although the exposed limestone cliffs and caves are a feature not of the Hamps but of the Manifold Valley.

River Manifold

The **River Manifold** like its neighbour, the River Dove, rises on Axe Edge and flows off the gritstone moors. Both run close together in deeply incised valleys as far as Longnor. The main packhorse route between Flash and Longnor is now tarmac covered and runs along the aptly named Edge Top, giving marvellous views down into the deep valley that carries the infant waters of the Manifold towards Longnor. Beyond the valley is the moor of Middle Hills and **Flash** village, the highest village in England.

Longnor is a compact village built of local stone mined at Daisy Knoll, on the Hollinsclough road. Even the bricks of the Crewe and Harpur Arms were made locally, at Reapsmoor, 3 miles (2.4km) to the south. Longnor is not at all pretentious, but it is none the worse for that. A recent development has been the small industrial estate near the fire station where clock manufacture is an unusual industry, but one not unknown to the region. Another surprising development on this site is **Upper Limits**, an indoor climbing wall, available to individuals proficient in rock climbing skills. For beginners and improvers there are courses or individual tuition. There are also facilities for archery here.

The village is a useful centre for exploring the upper reaches of the Manifold and Dove valleys. It has four pubs serving food, together with a very pleasant **Craft Centre** in the Market Hall, dated 1873, which retains its toll board for buyers and sellers at nineteenth-century Longnor markets and fairs. Cakes and snacks are available, including 'oaties'. Made in nearby Warslow, these have a variety of fillings in a traditional north Staffordshire oatcake. They are well worth a try! The centre has permanent displays of paintings by local artists, which are for sale.

Below Longnor the valley widens out into flat riverside meadows that are used for haymaking. Although it is not possible to walk down the valley to Longnor, below the village, paths and minor roads can be taken to walk to **Hulme End**.

Ahead lies the rounded form of **Ecton Hill**, heralding the start of the limestone and the more attractive section of the valley. At Ecton are the remains of the old copper mine. Today, the mines are quiet and the shafts flooded.

Many visitors wend their way to **Wetton Mill** and on to Thor's Cave, past limestone crags and the water swallets that take all the river water except in winter and periods of heavy rain. **Thor's Cave** rises 350 ft (107m) high above the river, its 60ft (18m) entrance a disappointing promise of a good cave system beyond.

Beyond **Weag's Bridge** is Beeston Tor, where the Manifold meets the Hamps. From here there is no path down the valley floor. A lane climbs from Ilam to Throwley, where the old hall remains have been stabilised and a path from Wetton to Castern cuts across the valley rim above the nature reserve. Both give glimpses into what must be the prettiest dale in the Peak without access to the public – and long may it remain so.

Beyond is Ilam country park owned by the National Trust, but best visited on the quiet days during the week rather than in the bustle of weekends and Bank Holidays. Below Ilam, the Dove flows down to Hanging Bridge on the outskirts of Ashbourne, which describes itself as 'The Gateway to Dovedale'.

Ashbourne

Ashbourne, (just a mile or so in Derbyshire) is the main town serving the area. Primarily a market town, it retains many eighteenth-century buildings together with other much older buildings in its main streets such as the Gingerbread Shop, which is timber framed and thought to be fifteenth-century. The Lamplight Restaurant in Victoria Square is of a similar age. Places to look out for in the town include the **Green Man and Black's Head Royal Hotel**. Its inn sign stretches over the street, and it has a small courtyard where coaches unloaded. Look at the Black's Head carved on the gallows-style inn sign; on one side he smiles, on the other he is sad. Of Georgian origin, the inn has associations with Boswell, who along with Dr Johnson stayed in the town with Dr Taylor who owned the Mansion in Church Street. Unfortunately, the 'Black's Head' in the name has recently been dropped. The Mansion is of seventeenth-century origin with a brick façade, and a porch similar to the Grey House opposite, dating from the mid-eighteenth century. Next door to the Mansion is the Old House, also built in the eighteenth century.

A walk along the street towards the church is very rewarding. There are many Georgian houses of interest including No 61, the Grey House, which is next to the Old Grammar School. Sir Nikolaus Pevsner described Church Street as one of the finest streets in Derbyshire. The Grammar School was founded in 1585. The central portion with four gables above was the old schoolroom and the school-masters' accommodation was at either side, while opposite are the almshouses built in 1614-30.

While in the street, visit **St Oswald's Church**, one of the grandest in the Peak, preferably in early spring when the churchyard is submerged beneath a carpet of daffodils. The oldest part of the existing building dates from the thirteenth century upon an earlier site, from which a Norman crypt has been located. The chancel was dedicated on the 24 April 1241, the date being recorded by the oldest known inscribed brass plate in the country. Most of the building dates from the fourteenth century. The spire rises to a height of 212 ft (65m).

The alabaster monuments in the church are especially notable, as well as a fine carving in marble of Penelope Boothby. The daughter of the owners of Ashbourne Hall was painted by Reynolds (this painting inspired the famous 'Bubbles' advert of Pear's Soap). The carving is by Banks and *(continued on p.36)*

The Market Hall, Longnor

Beresford Dale

Former grammar school, Ashbourne

Wetton

was exhibited at the Royal Academy. Penelope's death caused the breakup of her parent's marriage and the pitiful story became well known. It was quite common in Victorian times for little girls to attend fancy dress parties dressed as 'Penelope'. A guide book about the church is available.

Before moving on from Ashbourne, it is worth mentioning the village of **Norbury**, off the A515 road to Lichfield. About 5 miles (8km) down the Dove Valley from Ashbourne, it has a lovely church, which dates from the early fourteenth century. It is only just over the Staffordshire border. There is some armorial glass too, dating according to Pevsner from 1300-1307. The rear of the adjacent **Norbury Manor** dates from circa 1250 and was enlarged in 1305. It has been owned by the National Trust since 1987 and is open by appointment.

North of Ashbourne is **Alstonfield**, with a turning off the A515 opposite the former New Inns Hotel (now Holiday Fellowship owned). The village is situated on the limestone plateau, with many solid buildings closely knit together. The church contains seventeenth-century pews, a double-decker pulpit and a chest about 10ft (3m) long probably 700 years old. Part of the building is Norman.

In the village there is a good pub, the George Inn, well known to ramblers and tourists. From Alstonfield the road to Wetton descends down to Hope Dale. On the right is the Hope House Costume Museum and Restoration Workshop. Run by Notty Hornblower, the museum centres around Notty's extensive collection of some 300 cos-

tumes and 500 accessories. Although by appointment only, visitors may see clothes being restored in the workshop together with a display of costumes and accessories covering the period between 1840 and the 1970s.

Ilam village was rebuilt away from the Gothic Revival style hall in the early years of the nineteenth century. The hall was built for Mr Jesse Watts-Russell between 1821 and 1826, to the design of John Shaw. The formal buildings of Ilam Hall were demolished in 1935 and the remaining portion is now a youth hostel.

Ilam Hall, the church and the village school are all of interest. There is a National Trust shop, information centre and tea room in the stable block of the Watts-Russell house. The view from the terrace is magnificent and it is easy to see why Ilam Hall was built on this particular site. There are two Saxon crosses in the churchyard and inside the church is the tomb of St Bertram and Sir Francis Chantrey's statue of David Pike-Watts dated 1826. Notice the former Saxon doorway to the right of the porch. The former is very fine indeed and shows Jesse Watts-Russell's father-in-law on his death bed with his daughter and grandchildren at his bedside. The cross in the village near the bridge is dedicated to the daughter, Watts-Russell's wife, Mary.

The riverside walk takes you past the 'boil holes'. The first and larger one is where the River Manifold can be seen rising after its underground journey from Wetton Mill. The second and smaller boil hole contains the waters of the River Hamps. Other boil holes exist nearby where other water courses return to the surface.

Places to Visit

Hulme End

Manifold Valley Visitor Centre

Old Station buildings
☎ 01298 84679
Open: weekends throughout the year, school holidays and most days in the summer.
Information centre, exhibition on the history of the valley, picnic site.

Hartington

Hartington Cheese Shop

Market Place SK17 OAH
☎ 01298 84935
Open: daily, 9.30am-4.30pm, 5pm during Dec and 5.30pm during the summer. Closed 12.30-1pm for lunch.
Hartington Stilton available here.

Rookes Pottery

Mill Lane, Hartington SK17 OAN
☎ 01298 84650
www.rookespottery.co.uk
Open: weekdays 9.30am-4.30pm, Sat & Sun 10am-4pm. Closed in Jan & Feb.
Terracotta garden pottery made on the premises. Visitors may look round the workshop and see pots in production.

Longnor

Upper Limits

Unit 1, Buxton Road SK17 ONZ
☎ 01298 83149
Fax 01298 83857
www.leek.ac.uk/upper-limits
Open: Daily 10am-4pm, Mon, Wed and Fri evenings, 6pm-9.30pm.
Indoor climbing wall, climbing, caving and archery courses.

Longnor Craft Centre

The Market Hall, Market Square
☎ 01298 83587
Open: Mid-Feb to Christmas Eve daily 10am-5pm; Jan-mid-Feb, Fri-Sun only.
Exhibits and sale of work by local craftspeople and artists including traditional furniture. Coffee shop.

Alstonfield

Hope House Costume Museum and Restoration Workshop

DE6 2GE
☎ 01335 310318
www.hopehousemuseum.co.uk
By appointment only for groups. Over 300 items and 500 accessories of fashionable dress from late 18th century to 1970s.

Ilam

Ilam Country Park (National Trust)

5 miles (8km) north west of Ashbourne
☎ 01335 350549
Shop open: daily Apr-Oct 11am-5pm. Other weekends 11am-4pm (excluding Christmas and New Year)
Tearoom: mid-May-mid-Oct, Fri-Tue 11am-5pm, winter weekends 11am-4pm. Apr-mid-May weekends 11am-5pm.
84 acres of parkland on the banks of the River Manifold.

3. Stoke-on-Trent & Newcastle-under-Lyme

Newcastle is the oldest of these communities and retains its identity from Stoke-on-Trent, its larger neighbour. The two merge together in seamless union. Newcastle has existed for around a 1,000 years and its 'new castle' has long gone except for a few fragments. It had (and still has) far less industry than Stoke-on-Trent, although its last coalmine (Silverdale Colliery) only closed a few years ago. To the north, there was more coal working and marl extraction for brick and clay products, but little remains. Opencast coal working in the 1980s removed many traces of former coal working – even removing the main shaft of the Minnie Pit at Halmerend, where 155 men died in 1918.

Stoke-on-Trent is a relatively new-comer, being established in 1910 by an amalgamation of six towns – (from north to south) Tunstall, Burslem, Hanley, Stoke-on-Trent, Fenton and Longton. Just in case you thought that there were five towns, the confusion arises from Arnold Bennett's book *Five Towns*. He 'forgot' Fenton (as locals will tell you).

Stoke-on-Trent is usually better known as The Potteries. In fact it is the only urban area in the country named after its predominant industry – pottery manufacture. Along with coal extraction, the pits and the pots was a commonly used adjective for the area. Unfortunately all the deep mines have gone. One shallow mine, the former Apedale Colliery, is now a tourist attraction and English Heritage has spent a fortune at the former Chatterley Whitfield Colliery site, preserving what remains of its impressive array of buildings, steam engines etc. Here, as a reminder of the glory days of yesteryear, the colliery became the first in Europe to pass one million tons annual production. Access is not available however.

Many of the potteries (known locally as 'pot banks') have also closed and operations transferred to the Far East. Gone from The Potteries are the firms of Doulton, Spode, Minton, Johnson Brothers and many more. Wedgwood of course moved to a greenfield site many decades ago, to Barlaston, south of the city. Here it has an important visitor centre, exhibition hall, restaurant etc. A new £10m museum here opened in October 2008.

The Trent & Mersey Canal facilitated the easy movement of raw materials – china clay, flint etc and finished china and earthenware goods. The commercial traffic has gone, but the waterway now has leisure uses and also acts as a 'green lung' snaking its way through the city, as does its 'tributary' the Caldon Canal. The latter is particularly scenic where it runs along the Churnet Valley and many leisure boats make their slow way along to the recently refurbished wharf (long abandoned) at Froghall. Former flint mills at Etruria in the heart of the city and at Cheddleton (on the R. Churnet) are now preserved as visitor attractions alongside the canal. Flint was ground (either as lumps from chalk beds; or as chirt from seams in limestone beds) and the finely powdered rock used to harden chinaware, as a substitute for bone in 'bone china'.

A Victorian pottery, (built c. 1856) complete with its bottle kilns, survives at **Gladstone Pottery Museum**, in Uttoxeter Road, Longton.

Apparently there once was some 2,000 bottle kilns, belching out smoke across the city, but only a handful can now be found. Here one can see how our forefathers and mothers worked long hours at benches crafting everything from the finest china ornaments to the humble teacup and toilet. It is a working museum and you can try your hand at the potter's wheel.

Today much redevelopment continues apace, old factories and terraced streets being replaced by new housing and modern business parks. The main shopping area for the region is at Hanley, its main streets home to the usual multiples, although some firms have sites elsewhere, such as Next at Tunstall. Hanley is ringed by an inner-ring road and many car parks and also has what is described as the 'Cultural Quarter' of the city. Here is the **Museum & Art Gallery**, housing the world's finest china and porcelain collection, although much of it is not on show.

The museum also houses a Spitfire fighter aircraft, a memorial to Reginald Mitchell, its designer, who was born locally. Just around the corner in Albion Street is **Bethesda Methodist Chapel** of 1819, saved in the nick of time to preserve its fine interior. It featured on the TV programme '*Restoration*' which highlighted the plight of the building's decay.

Some of the remaining potteries have factory shops but, there is only one major commercially operating pottery visitor centre, being Wedgwood with its new museum. You can also try your hand at the potter's wheel and have a tour of the factory, seeing the manufacturing process first hand. There is also a large restaurant and shop to round off your visit.

There are several other, varied, attractions for the visitor, but let us finish off those concerned with industry in days gone by. Two are to be found tucked away, if not off the beaten track. At the junction of the Trent & Mersey Canal and the Caldon Canal is The **Etruria Industrial Museum**. Here bones and flint were formerly ground to powder and used to make bone china. The old steam engine survives in working order. A new museum building compliments the 1820s engine, which may be seen in steam on the first weekend of every month from June to December. Interactive activities including craft activities

keep the children occupied and happy on this interesting canal-side location.

More ambitious was the conversion of the last coal mine in the area into a museum at **Apedale Heritage Centre**. It had an incline instead of a shaft and underground tours take you down to the coal seams where over 100 men used to work. Exhibition galleries on the local coal industry, the miners and their way of life have been carefully crafted into an absorbing attraction. There is even a section on the nearby Roman fort at Holditch, which illustrates well the point that there is much more to this place than just coal. To find it follow 'Apedale Valley' brown signs from Chesterton to the Apedale Community Country Park. The Centre is at the end of Loomer Road, just inside the 450-acre country park of woodland, wetland and meadow. If you intend going underground, remember to take warm clothes and sensible footwear.

Gardens to Visit

As a contrast to the heady expression of working life in days gone by is the heady scent of a beautiful garden being experienced today and around Stoke-on-Trent, if not in it, are some really good ones. To the east is Consall Hall garden, over 70-acres of artistic composition, designed, created and nursed along by William Podmore on the site of a Victorian colliery adjacent to his family home. How this garden developed and what there is to see is described on p.51.

To the north is the nationally known **Biddulph Grange Garden**. It was *(continued on p.44)*

Above and bottom-left: Biddulph Grange Garden (N.T.); bottom-right: Bridestones, Bosley Cloud

Above: Trent and Mersey Canal, Etruria Industrial Museum

created by James Bateman in the early 1840s when he built the adjacent mansion in Italian Renaissance style. The garden had different themes, such as Italian, Egyptian and Chinese. All had become seriously overgrown and in some places even filled in when it was acquired by the National Trust, who painstakingly restored it. This is a lovely garden with many surprises. It is a superb example of early-Victorian garden layout and covers many acres. It is popular too, especially on sunny weekends, but do not allow this to put you off. A visit here is definitely recommended.

Just six miles (9km) away and just over the Cheshire border is **Little Moreton Hall**, owned by the National Trust. The knot garden there is nowhere near as large as Biddulph Grange of course, but the two places make for a very interesting day out. Little Moreton is perhaps the finest surviving black and white timbered house in Cheshire. It is Tudor in age and exhibits craftsmanship at it finest.

Whilst out of the county, another small garden is also worth a visit in spring if time permits. It is **Harehill Garden**, now in the hands of the National Trust. It is between Macclesfield and Alderley Edge. To get to it from Alderley Edge, take the B5087 to Macclesfield. Turn north onto Prestbury Road for ¾-mile and the entrance is on the left.

The garden is adjacent to a private house and was a clear labour of love. The entrance path is long and lined with some of the 70 species of rhododendrons to be seen here. The main garden feature being within a high wall,

affording shelter, serenity and cover beneath a pergola's roof.

Beyond is a wooded area, with a large pool and woodland walks. This is not a very big site but in its own way, a little gem.

The house at Biddulph Grange is now divided into upmarket apartments, which prevents a tour of the building – long used as an orthopaedic hospital and therefore well known to many former workers, patients and visitors. Trentham Hall has been demolished and one of the nation's significant architectural gems has been lost, but the gardens and grounds remain (see below).

One house which may be visited close to Stoke is **Whitmore Hall** and it is well worth it, although your visit has to be in the summer. Situated 4 miles (7km) from Newcastle-under-Lyme on the Shrewsbury road (A53), this well appointed Grade 1 listed building is a fine example of a Carolinian Manor House, built in 1676. It is, however, encasing a much earlier building and the owners, the Mainwaring family and their ancestors have been living on this site for over 900 years. It really is a lovely house and should not be missed.

Whitmore Hall garden is best visited when the rhododendrons and masses of bluebells are in flower. The late 18th century park includes a large lake and a later maze of 1842. The stables are described as a rare Elizabethan example, one of the oldest in the country. Pevsner dates them to 1620-30, the horse boxes being 'perfectly preserved, with rustic columns of wood and wooden arches with big globular pendants'. The arches are repeated at the rear of the stalls too.

It all adds to the surprise and appreciation of a lovely hall and its estate.

From Whitmore, it is only a few minutes ride to **Trentham Estate**, the site of the former splendid hall and former home of the Duke of Sutherland. The latter left when the estate was being threatened by urban sprawl from the city and the smell of pollution in the River Trent.

Charles Barry built the house in 1834 in Italianate-style for the 2nd Duke. A further phase of building followed in the 1840s.

Pevsner explains that the Italianate villa-type was created by Nash at Cronkhill in c. 1802. Jeffrey Wyatville produced the grandest example of the style at Chatsworth in the 1820s, when the 357ft (108m) long north wing was built for the 6th Duke of Devonshire. However, Trentham was superb and Pevsner describes it as 'in its own way, architecturally as important as the Houses of Parliament'. Prince Albert copied the style of Trentham at Osborne on the Isle of Wight and a fashionable 'new' style of architecture took off.

By 1910, the Duke's descendant had tired of the 'appalling smell' from the river and offered the building to the County Council and Borough of Stoke-on-Trent. They declined it and a national gem fell under the demolition man's hammer. Part of the west wing and the stable block remained. For years it was a low key attraction but a recent and substantial investment has seen the emergence of a major new attraction (see p.48).

Smaller, but captivating is the **Dorothy Clive Garden** at Blackbrook near Maer. A couple of miles beyond Baldwin's Gate on the A53 Newcastle-Shrewsbury road is a staggered junction with the A51 Stone-Chester road. Upon joining the A51, don't turn left on the A53 but continue north for about a mile or so. The garden is then on your right. Originally, it was set in a former sandstone quarry, where there is an emphasis of a woodland setting with rhododendrons etc, woodland paths and a careful use of water. Now the area between the A51 and the wood has also been incorporated into the garden with large herbaceous borders, shrubs, ornamental trees etc.

It compliments the earlier work wonderfully. The garden is administered by a trust; is not as well known as perhaps it ought to be and well worth visiting in the spring and summer.

One particular garden eye-catcher has become a well known county landmark. It is **Mow Cop 'Castle'**, near Biddulph. It is a folly, portraying a ruined 'castle' tower and an adjoining arch and may be seen from many miles away. It was built by Randle Wilbraham of **Rode Hall**, Scholar Green, in Cheshire. Here the garden is open to the public, enabling you to see what Mow Cop's folly looked like from the home of the man that built it in 1754 – one of the earliest examples of a recreation of a castle ruin as a folly. Mow Cop is where the Primitive Methodist Movement (known as the Prims) was founded in 1810 by Hugh Bourne and William Clowes. It eventually united with the Wesleyan Methodist movement.

Monkey Forest, Trentham, with nearly 150 Barbary Apes in a 65 acre park. They ignore you as you cannot take food in with you!

Above: Interior, Whitmore Hall,

Right: The stables, Whitmore Hall

Above: Whitmore Hall from the park

Trentham Estate

'Creating exceptional days out for everyone'

In the early 1970s, the highlight at Alton Towers was a column which rotated with a rope hanging down from it. Then the thrill rides of the theme park arrived and visitors came in their tens of thousands. Drayton Manor Park and Biddulph Grange Garden followed, enhancing the county's reputation for tourism, expressed through fun and culture.

Slumbering on was Trentham Gardens, attracting visitors but nothing too exciting. Now, given vision and investment, that has changed and the county has an incredible new visitor attraction – Trentham Estate (with the Wedgwood Museum opening too at nearby Barlaston).

Having pulled up at the roundabout on the A34 with the Trentham-Longton road, you can turn into the North Gate or continue south to South Gate for the Monkey Forest (see p46): there are in fact three attractions here. At North Gate is the Retail Village, where you can browse in a street of shops ranging from candle making, fudge indulgence to good clothing outlets. The 60 shops here will soon be doubled. Off the street is the entrance to the Italianate Garden, the third attraction. St Modwen Properties, the owners, claim to be "creating exceptional days out for everyone" and Trentham Estate is just that. In addition to the variety of the shops (situated next to your car park) is the UK's largest garden centre. It's bold, huge and if it is just plants you are after, a good range too.

You will be dazzled by just the entrance with its canal pond feature leading you in from the entrance to a circular, balustraded balcony reflecting the Italianate-style of the former mansion. It dominates the middle of this huge shopping and dining experience developed by retail group Blue Diamond in association with Trentham Estate.

The Italianate Garden, off the Retail Village, is by far the major attraction here and is set to become one of the UK's leading tourism attractions. It has two parts, the Upper Flower Garden, following the restoration of Charles Barry's garden which he designed along with the now demolished Italianate mansion in the 1830s. It is, however, the Lower Flower Garden which is so exciting; it is an awesome, overwhelming gardening experience. Designed by Dutch landscape designer, Piet Oudolf, it covers a 10-acre site below the Upper Flower Garden and beside the lake.

Set against a background of the park, with its mature trees including oak and cedar, it is the bold and imaginative planting by Tom Stuart-Smith (6-times RHS Chelsea gold medal winner) which takes your breath away. Mind you, using 76,000 plants and 100,000 bulbs does help. Here is an all-year garden with ever changing vistas as you walk around the 70 flower beds with views to the park, Barry's loggia, the lake and bronze statue of Perseus and Medusa etc.

It is not only good, however, it is a quiet, tranquil garden; there are no signs saying 'keep the children off the grass'either. Trentham want you to enjoy this experience and come back in the following season when the colours are different. Moreover, the Trentham Experience does not end here.

You can take a five-mile walk around the lake; a boat ride on the mile-long lake itself, or explore Capability Brown's parkland, including the country's first Bare-foot walk to invigorate your feet before showering them off and wandering on into the 750-acre estate. Young children are well catered for and a natural amphitheatre, the Teatro del Lago (Theatre by the Lake) is used for cultural events. Additionally there are many events going on all the time. Ask about this at the Reception desk or ring ahead.

St Modwen to date have spent £70m here, but future developments do not end with the Retail Village. A bold and imaginative development promises to be as equally exciting as the Italianate Garden. A 5-star hotel is to be built on the site of the former house, and also refurbishing its Italianate-style remains, a style so popular in Victorian England following Barry's work here and its use at Osborne House by Prince Albert. It will follow the recently opened lodge-style Premier Inn on the estate.

Taking the investment to £100m, Trentham is becoming one of the finest attractions in the country. Situated close to the M6 (junction 15), access could not be easier. Exceptional days out for everyone are promised and delivered. Staffordshire is now becoming a premier tourist destination in the UK.

Having said all this, the third attraction area here is on top of the above. Monkey Forest is situated on a 65-acre site at the south end of the lake and adjacent to Aerial Extreme.

For photographs of Trentham Estate, see pp38 & 44.

Top: Wedgwood Museum, Barlaston; above-left: Black Basalt vases and right The Apotheosis of Homer vase, c. 1790, both scenes at The Wedgwood Museum

The Churnet Valley was always referred to locally as the 'Secret Valley' until the canal reopened and the steam trains started. However, within the valley area was a garden that was even more secretive – a garden that has been 50 years in the making. William Podmore and his late wife Edna developed a 70-acre landscape garden at **Consall Hall**. The surprise is that most of the views contain an eye-catcher and the view itself consists of a composition. It is like looking at a living painting. In fact William painted each scene as he wanted it and planting followed the painting.

All the paths are tarmaced, there are five lakes – one covering a Victorian coalmine – and work continues at a pace even now. The garden is now open to the public and so it needs to be. It is an amazing achievement and one of the county's main attractions.

Just to the south of Consall is the **Foxfield Railway**. It is one of the few industrial railways in the country still in continuous use, with steam locos pulling trains nearly three miles down the line to the former Foxfield Colliery. The railway is home to about 30 locos at Caverswall Road Station, Blithe Bridge. Steam trains run every Wednesday from April to October. There are lots of events and the line compliments the longer line of the North Staffordshire railway based at Cheddleton.

Other Attractions

The centre of Hanley has two (one each) of the county's major theatres and concert halls. The **Victoria Hall**, at the rear of Hanley Town Hall has a well-used Victorian Concert Hall, as well as the Tourist Information Centre and Atrium Café Bar (open daily). There is a further theatre in Newcastle-under-Lyme.

A few minutes walk from the Victoria Hall is Piccadilly, one of Hanley's main shopping streets and the home to the **Regent Theatre**. Now restored, it offers a high quality programme of opera, national ballet and West End musicals. Over at Festival Park, Etruria is the Odeon multiplex cinema and in Leek Road, between the bottom of Lichfield Street and Station Road is **The Rep**.

Newcastle also has a **Museum and Art Gallery** at The Firs in The Brampton. It was built in 1855 and the architect was Charles Lynam. There are usually several exhibitions on display together with a gallery of paintings collected over the years portraying Newcastle in days gone by.

Tucked away at Smallthorne, about halfway between Burslem and Norton (to the east), is **Ford Green Hall**. It was described by Pevsner as a lovely timber-framed house with a two-bay Georgian addition. Built by William Ford in c. 1580 and altered over the years, it had a Georgian edition in c. 1734. Having become dilapidated, it was purchased by the City Corporation in 1946 for £1,100.00. After considerable restoration work, it opened as a folk museum in 1952.

There is clearly much to interest visitors to the north-west of the county, more than one might expect in fact. If you do wish to move north through the built-up area, use the A34 for the quickest route, or the A500, known locally as the D-road (the shape it makes with the M6).

County Parks & Greenways

1. Leek to Rushton Spencer Greenway
Surfaced former railway line from Leek towards Macclesfield, 5m/8km long, runs past Rudyard lake. Car park at Rudyard former station and at north end of Lake. Miniature railway from the car park. Toilets and cafe at west side of the lake dam.

2. Stafford to Newport Greenway
Former railway line extending to 8.75 miles/14km. Part of the Staffs County Council Way for the Millennium which crosses the county from east to west. Horse riding permits available (www.staffordshire.gov.uk/environment/e-land/countryside.openspaces for application form for horse riding permits).

3. Oakamoor to Denstone Greenway
4.4 miles/7km of former Churnet Valley Railway, mostly well surfaced. Horse riding permit available (see 2 above). Car park at Oakamoor Country park which is adjacent to the line. Look out for remains of the former Uttoxeter Canal especially below Alton. It closed in 1847.

Oakamoor Country Park
15.5ac/6.27ha – site of copper and brass works. About half of the copper for the first transatlantic cable was made here in 1857 and nearly all the UK's tram wiring. Car park/toilets.

4. Greenway Bank Country Park
114ac/46ha with large lake providing water to the Caldon/Trent and Mersey Canals. Woodland trails ablaze with rhododendrons etc in spring. Visitor Centre open weekends (Sun pm in Winter), car park/toilets. 2 miles/3.2km from Biddulph.

5. Deep Hayes Country Park, Denford, nr Leek
143ac/58ha site with woodland and pools, visitor centre and toilets (open weekends – Sun pm only in Winter). Former site of reservoir drained when judged unsafe.

6. Apedale Country Park, Chesterton
Large site 454ac/184ha of open meadow, woodland and pools. Adjacent is the Apedale Colliery Museum (see p41). Horse riding permitted (see 2 above re: permit).

7. Consall Nature Park
Large woodland area with lots of trails and boardwalks across boggy areas. A site of special scientific interest. Visitor Centre open weekends (Sun pm only in winter). Leaflet available showing the trails.

8. Froghall Wharf
Former transhipment wharfs where limestone was loaded onto narrowboats. Picnic area, parking, toilets and kiosk selling drinks, ice cream etc. Recently reopened lower wharf with moorings. Situated off Foxt Road.

9. Hanchurch Hills
2 Miles/3.2km west of Trentham. Three circular walks (2 to 7 miles/3 to 11km long), picnic site.

10. Hanbury Common
Picnic area with good views over the Lower Dove Valley. Fauld Crater (see p.73). South east of Draycott in the Clay.

11. Cannock Chase Country Park
See p.61 re: the Country Park and Cannock Chase Visitor Centre.

12. Highgate Common Country Park
230ac/94ha, north of Kinver. Open heathland and woodland with three trails of about one hour's duration.

13. Kinver Edge
See p.84 for details of this area.

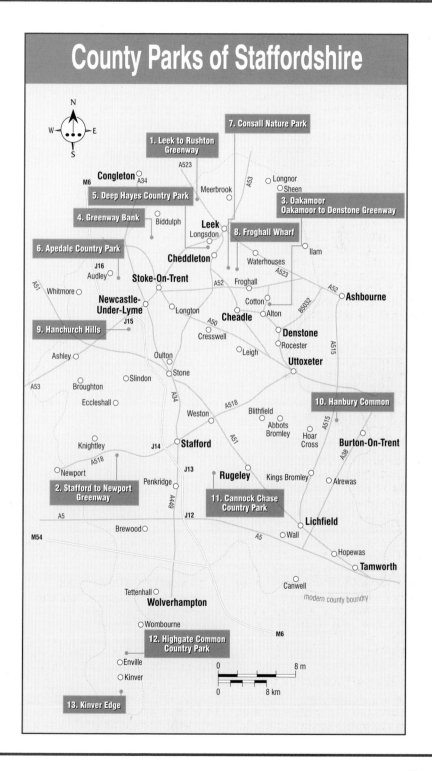

County Parks of Staffordshire

N
W E
S

7. Consall Nature Park

1. Leek to Rushton Greenway

A523

Congleton A34
M6

5. Deep Hayes Country Park

Meerbrook
Longnor
Sheen
A53

3. Oakamoor Oakamoor to Denstone Greenway

4. Greenway Bank

Biddulph

Leek
Longsdon

8. Froghall Wharf

6. Apedale Country Park

Cheddleton
Waterhouses
Ilam

J16
Audley
Stoke-On-Trent
A52 Froghall
A523

A51
Whitmore
Cotton
A52 Ashbourne

Newcastle-Under-Lyme
Longton
A50
Cheadle
Alton
B5032

9. Hanchurch Hills
J15
Cresswell
Denstone
Rocester

Ashley
Oulton
Leigh
Uttoxeter

A53
Broughton
Slindon
Stone

Eccleshall

A34
Weston
A518
Blithfield

A515

10. Hanbury Common

Knightley
Abbots Bromley
Hoar Cross
A515

A518
J14
Stafford
A51
Burton-On-Trent

Newport
J13
Rugeley
A38

2. Stafford to Newport Greenway
Penkridge
Kings Bromley
Alrewas

A5
A449
J12

11. Cannock Chase Country Park

Brewood
Lichfield

M54
A5
Wall
Hopewas

Tamworth

Canwell

modern county boundary

Tettenhall
Wolverhampton

Wombourne
M6

12. Highgate Common Country Park

Enville
0   8 m

Kinver
0   8 km

13. Kinver Edge

Country Parks in the north of the County

Biddulph Grange Country Park

Situated adjacent to Biddulph Grange Garden (National Trust)), this park centres on the former lake in the grounds to the estate. There are a number of waymarked trails and some are made for wheelchair access, others involving steeper gradients. If you fancy fishing you can buy a ticket, available from the Visitor Centre. Guided walks are available on certain dates.

Visitor Centre/Café – open weekends and bank holidays except out of season, 10am-4pm.

☎ 01782 522447

For fishing enquiries ☎ 01538 483579

Greenway Bank Country Park

This park is south of Biddulph Grange Country Park and east of Brindley Ford. It is based on the site of Greenway Bank a demolished country house, although some out-buildings remain and now form the estate yard and Visitor Centre. The park encompasses the adjacent Knypersley Pool that supplies water to the Trent & Mersey Canal, together with the estate of Greenway Bank and adjacent Knypersley Hall. There are paths along the side of the Knypersley Pool (in fact a reservoir) and the lake above it. The area is particularly attractive in spring when the rhododendrons are in flower. Above Knypersley Pool can be seen the source of the River Trent.

Visitor Centre

☎ 01782 518200

Long Distance Trails

Biddulph is the start of the **Biddulph Valley Way** and also the Gritstone Trail. The former is the old Biddulph-Congleton railway line and starts from Brindley Ford, south of Biddulph and runs up the valley before cutting across to Congleton. The **Gritstone Trail** starts at Kidsgrove and runs for 35miles (56km) to Disley. It has now been split into three sections for easier walking. The first section extends to Timbersbrook, on the west flank of Bosley Cloud, the large outcrop at the edge of the Cheshire Plain.

Starting in Mow Cop is the Staffordshire Way that runs down the length of the county to its southern tip at Kinver. It initially heads north-east before turning to head south-east on part of the Macclesfield-Leek railway line before heading down the west side of Rudyard Reservoir.

Both the Gritstone Trail and the **Staffordshire Way** follow the same route along a pronounced ridge offering panoramic views before descending to join the Biddulph Valley Way, leaving the latter on the outskirts of Congleton to head for Bosley Cloud.

Festivals

Stoke-on-Trent Ceramics Festival – October
info: www.stokeceramicsfestival.co.uk
Leek Arts Festival – May*
Newcastle-under-Lyme Jazz & Blues Festival – May*
*For information ☎ local Tourist Information Centre

Top-left: Ford Green Hall, Smallthorne; top-right: Dorothy Clive Garden, Willoughbridge; middle: Trentham Estate Retail Village; bottom: Little Morton Hall, near Congleton

Places to Visit

Waterworld
Festival Park, Festival Way
Stoke-on-Trent ST1 5PY
☎ 01782 205747
www.waterworld.co.uk
Please telephone for opening times
Ⓟ & ♨ ☂

Wedgwood Visitor Centre
Barlaston, Stoke-on-Trent ST12 9ES
☎ 0870 606 1759
www.thewedgwoodvisitorcentre.com
Open: weekdays, 9am-5pm; weekends,
10am-5pm
Factory part of trip: excludes Friday pm or
weekends. Check trips in August
Ⓟ & ♨ ☂

Trentham Monkey Forest
Stone Road, Trentham ST4 8AY
www.monkey-forest.com
Ⓟ ♨ ☂

Aerial Extreme
Stone Entrance, Trentham ST4 8AY
www.aerialextreme.co.uk
'Thrills without limits' adventure ropes
course.
Ⓟ ♨ (reduced for<16)

Ford Green Hall
Ford Green Road, Smallthorne ST6 1NG
☎ 01782 233195
www.stoke.gov.uk/museums
Open: Sun-Thurs, 1-5pm (except Xmas-
New Year)
Ⓟ ♨ (family ticket) ☂

Potteries Museum & Art Gallery
Bethesda St, Hanley ST1 3DW
☎ 01782 232323

www.gov.uk/museums
Open: times vary (telephone)
Ⓟnearby & ♨ (free) ☂

Gardens

Biddulph Grange (N.T.)
Grange Road, Biddulph ST8 75D
☎ 01782 517999
Open: Easter–end-Oct, Wed-Sun, 11am-5pm
Ⓟ & (partly) ♨ (family ticket)

Consall Hall Landscape Gardens
Consall, Wetley Rocks ST9 OAG
☎ 01782 551947
www.consallgardens.co.uk
Open: Wed, Sun, Bank Hol. Mon 10am-
5pm from Good Fri–30th Sep.
70 acres of landscaped garden. Teas.
Ⓟ & ♨

Dorothy Clive Garden
Willoughbridge, Market Drayton TF9 4EU
☎ 01630 647237
Open: Mar-Oct, 10am-5.30pm
Ⓟ & ♨ (reduced for<16)

Trentham Estate
Stone Road, Trentham ST4 8AX
☎ 01782 646646
www.trentham.co.uk
Open: gardens open daily (except Xmas Day)
Ⓟ & ♨ ☂

Whitmore Hall
Whitmore, Newcastle-under-Lyme ST5 5HW
☎ 01782 680478
Open: garden with house, 1st May-31st Aug,
Tues & Wed, 2-5pm
Ⓟ ♨ (children 50p) ☂

Little Morton Hall (N.T.)
Nr Congleton, Cheshire CW12 4SD
☎ 01260 272018

Open: end–Mar-Oct, Wed-Sun, 11.30am-
5pm; early-Mar, Nov, Dec 1.30am-4pm
℗ ⅲ (<17 discount, < 5 free) ☞

Industrial History/ Pottery Outlets

Apedale Heritage Centre

Loomer Road, Chesterton
Newcastle-under-Lyme, ST5 7RR
☎ 07837 225790
www.apedale.heritage.cwc.net
Open: museum, café & shop, daily
10.30am-4pm. Underground visits, Sat,
Sun & BH Mondays 10.30am-3pm
Weekday visits by appointment only
℗ ♿ (not underground) ⅲ (but children <5
not underground) ☞

Etruria Industrial Museum

Bedford St, Etruria, ST4 7AF (Sat Nav ref:
ST1 4RB)
☎ 01782 233144
www.stoke.gov.uk/museums
Museum, potter's mill, tearoom, shop
Open: Wed-Sun, 12-4.30pm
Britain's last remaining steam-powered
potter's mill and new museum
℗ ♿ ⅲ (family ticket) ☞

Gladstone Pottery Museum

Uttoxeter Road, Longton
☎ 01782 237777
www.stoke.gov.uk/gladstone
Open: daily, all year, 10am-5pm except
Xmas
℗ ♿ ⅲ (family ticket) ☞

Dudson Pottery Museum

Hope Street, Hanley, ST1 5DD
☎ 01782 285286

www.dudson.com
19th century pottery with bottle oven
Open: Mon-Fri, 10am-3pm
℗ ⅲ (free) ☞

Dudson Factory

Nile Street, Burslem, ST6 2BA
☎ 01782 821075
Open: Mon-Fri, 9am-5pm, Sat 9am-
12noon

Royal Stafford Tableware

Wedgwood Place
Burslem, ST6 4EE
☎ 01782 525419
Pottery factory outlet and ceramic café
experience – create your own design and
have it fired.
♿ ☞

Theatres

Victoria Hall

Bagnall St, Hanley ST1 3AD
☎ 0870 060 6649
www.victoria-hall.info

Regent Theatre

Piccadilly, Hanley ST1 1AP
☎ 0870 060 6649
www.regenttheatre.co.uk

New Vic Theatre

Etruria Road, Newcastle ST5 0JG
☎ 01782 717962
www.newvictheatre.org.uk

Mitchell Memorial Theatre

Broad St, Hanley ST1 4HG
☎ 01782 235411
www.stoke.gov.uk/mitchelltheatre

The Rep

Leek Road, Stoke-on-Trent
☎ 01782 209784

4. Stafford and Cannock Chase

Halfway down the A34 between Stoke and Stafford – a distance of 12 miles (19km) – is **Stone**. It is actually bi-passed by this arterial route, a fortunate providence. It had an Augustinian Priory in c. 1135 and was created a borough in1251, which included a right to a (Tuesday) market. Staffordshire was well-blessed with medieval boroughs, only five other counties having more by the mid 14th century.

Above: Stafford Castle; above right: Ancient High House, Stafford

A reminder of the Priory has survived at a house called The Priory in Lichfield Street, south of the town centre. Here remains part of the undercroft with a rib-vaulted roof. However it was not until Georgian times that the town began to grow in importance. It had been conveniently positioned on the road to the north west, Carlisle and Scotland. The development of turnpike roads improved old coach routes and found Stone still on the road north and one of its better buildings, The Crown Inn, survives in the High Street. It was built in 1778 and is one of several quality brick buildings in the town which date from Georgian times.

The **Trent and Mersey Canal** was constructed just to the west of the High Street and brought new developments with a wharf serving the canal. The shoemaking and beer businesses in the town would also have benefited from the new transport system, especially when the canal was connected to other canals heading for Birmingham and Stourport (for the River Severn). In time, the canals were overtaken by the railways and Stone found itself favourably situated for a third time when one of the main north west routes was built through the town.

A walk around Stone

Some PR agency seems to have dreamed up the name of 'Canal Town' for Stone. It's more romantic than railways one supposes. It does remind one of those former times and the Jacobean-style railway station is a reminder not only of Victorian commercial confidence, but of the similar style buildings at Winton Square at Stoke-on-Trent station. A walk along the canal should be considered, not only to see old, refurbished canal side warehouses, but the Star Inn, conveniently situated by Star Lock, where you can watch narrowboats glide past and soak up the atmosphere as well as a drink. The pub pre-dates the canal and a plaque records the opening of the latter.

A town trial leaflet is available, which highlights places of interest. Now, as in most places, traditional industries have gone, the large Lotus and Delta shoe factory on the A520 road to Meir has closed and John Joules's brewery, established in 1780, only survived for four years once it had been acquired by Bass in 1970. Joules (pronounced Jules) 'Stone' bitter has since been 'replicated', but the reincarnation does not quite produce the distinctive, previously experienced taste – a great pity, despite it being a worthy cask ale.

A recent innovation has been the establishment of a new brewery in part of the former Bent's Brewery in the town. One ale is currently being produced – called Lymestone. Look out also for The Exchange Inn, near the Police Station. It has recently re-opened and is run by Titanic Brewery of Stoke-on-Trent (Titanic's master, Captain Smith came from Stoke-on-Trent).

Stone is well worth stopping off to explore and can be linked to a visit to Wedgwood's Pottery just to the north of the town.

The little village of **Barlaston** is also home to the Wedgwood Pottery. There is a long drive down to it and look out for the elegant **Barlaston Hall**, situated to the south east of the pottery, restored by English Heritage after years on their Buildings at Risk Register.

Thinking of water for brewing (above), reminds one of the need for water for domestic consumption in general. To the west of Stone, are two very distinctive water **pumping works** at **Swynnerton** and **Millmeece**. The latter retains its steam-operated pumping engines, two horizontal tandem compounds, although no longer in service. They were the last of this type in use for pumping water and were only taken out of service in 1980. They are open to the public at Millmeece from time to time. Swynnerton is not open but the building is quite striking and worth the detour to see.

To the south of Swynnerton and east of Eccleshall is **Izaak Walton's Cottage**. He was born in Stafford in 1575 and lived in this cottage later in life. Famous for his *'Compleat Angler'*, still in print 3-400 years later, this timber-framed cottage is open to the public in the summer months. It is at Shallowford, close to the electrified railway line between London and the north-west. Picnic facilities are available in the garden.

Stafford

Twenty years after Walton's birth, a large timber-framed building was built in Greengate Street, Stafford. It still survives and is now the largest timber-framed town house to survive in England, a remarkable treasure for the county town. It now houses the **Ancient High House Museum** on its upper floors (the ground floor is occupied by a couple of shops).

The rooms are given over to various themes. Charles I and his nephew and leader of his army, Prince Rupert, stayed here and there is a Civil War Room. Later generations are represented with a Victorian and Edwardian Rooms, etc. The attic houses the Staffordshire Yeomanry Regiment Museum. A later visitor was Charles Darwin, who stayed two doors away at the equally ancient Swan Inn in 1852.

Much older and situated to the west of the town, close to the M6 motorway, is **Stafford Castle**. This was a large fortified site incorporating a former medieval village and a large bailey on which a stone keep was built in 1348. Like many castles, it was partially demolished by Cromwell after the Civil War. However in 1813 a Gothic-Revival house was built on the foundations and was used as a house for 150 years. It fell into disrepair after that and the council wished to demolish it altogether. Fortunately this did not happen and enough remains of the building to gain a good idea of how the castle would have looked, let alone the later house. There is a Visitor Centre now just off the Newport road and adjacent to the outer motte or defensive rampart. The views from the castle are extensive on a good day.

Stafford is not too large a town and it has a good atmosphere as a shopping centre. The River Sow meanders through the town centre; it lends a seeming calming influence on the place. Backed by elegant properties intermingling with the shops, Stafford is simply a nice place to visit. For the historians it is worth noting that **St. Mary's Church** and its neighbour **St. Chad's** are of Norman foundation. The town has not only the County's Record Office, but also the adjacent William Salt Library with an excellent collection of paintings, drawings and documents on the county.

Greengate Street, with the Ancient High House and **Swan Inn**, runs into the Market Square, a large open area dominated by the former **Shire Hall** of 1798, with its Palladian front. This whole area (and street) is pedestrianised, making for stress-free shopping. Behind Market Square is Market Street and the Tourist Information Centre. It dispenses a Town Trail leaflet; its comprehensive enough, but frustratingly hard to read.

Cannock Chase

At the time of the Norman Conquest, much of the southern half of the county was forested, with three great forests in particular – Brewood, Kinver and Cannock. This area was extended to the north of Stafford, covering the areas now occupied by the Potteries and Newcastle and stretching across to reach the edge of the Staffordshire Moorland moors. Yet another large forest existed at Needwood, north-west of what is now Burton-on-Trent.

The majority of this forested area, which would have been a mixture of forest, heathland and some human occupation has now gone; stripped away to create agricultural land or for fuel. The two main trees were the oak and the holly. The former provided fuel and timber, the latter provided winter forage for needy animals. Holly and Hollin place names are a reminder of this, especially in areas away from settlements.

Cannock Chase is a large tract of the former Cannock Forest, although in reality, a rump of what it had been. It is basically a large estate, admittedly having suffered from some encroachment. Rights of hunting were given by the Crown to the Bishop of Lichfield and his successors in 1290. They were relieved of the land by the plundering activities of Henry VIII, who gave it to one of his retainers, William Paget, whose descendant became the Marquis of Anglesey. Paget exploited iron reserves on the Chase and cut down vast acreages of timber to feed the furnaces. His descendants lived at Beaudesert, a large country seat, sited on the Bishop's hunting lodge, down the generations, until they moved to another family estate, Plas Newydd on Anglesey where they still live.

In Victorian times and up until comparatively recently, coal reserves were wrought, creating a destructive industrial landscape on the Chase. This was augmented by the military, with a huge Great War hospital and later, a RAF Camp. The last of the mines closed in 1993 and the hospital and RAF camp have also gone now.

Today, much of the area is owned by Forestry Enterprise (who planted large

Top-left: Cannock Chase; right: Museum of Cannock Chase, Hednesford;
bottom: The working farm at Shugborough with a Staffordshire waggon

tracts with pine instead of oak), and the County Council. Between the two of them, they deserve to take a bow for making the Chase a huge recreational area, sensitively structured, not only across one of the largest surviving areas of lowland heathland in the country, but an AONB (Area of Outstanding Natural Beauty) extending to some 25 sq. miles.

There are way marked trails for walkers and cyclists in abundance and even a waymarked trail all the way from Hednesford railway station to the **Cannock Chase Visitor Centre**. The latter is one of three on the Chase with good facilities for visitors generally and the family specifically. These also include Birches Valley Forest Centre and the Wolseley Centre by the A51 southeast of Little Haywood.

The **Birches Valley Forest Centre** has a **Go Ape!** attraction. This high wire forest adventure is one of a growing number of such locations across the country. There is another at Pooles Cavern, Buxton, just over the Stafford-shire county boundary and Trentham Estate has a similar attraction.

These centres are augmented by many car parks discreetly sited to maximise access and the **Museum of Cannock Chase**, situated on the site of Valley Colliery off the Hednesford - Rugeley road (A460) just north of Hednesford.

The A.O.N.B. was created in 1958 because of its landscape value, wildlife and long history. Its landscape contrasts ancient oak woods with pine forest, parklands and greenfields with sand-stone heathland with a mixture of grass, heather, gorse, shrubs and birch. Here you can mingle with the crowds at the Visitor Centres; set off with boots or bike; find peace and quiet and a variety of wildlife that includes various species of deer. Forestry Enterprise even manages a herd of c.400 deer on its estate. They maintain a practice established by the Bishops of Lichfield over 800 years ago. Draining the western side of the chase is the Sher Brook. Here in its tranquil valley you may well get a glimpse of these timid animals.

The number of visitors, together with pressures on land use, e.g. an increase of the use of the area by horses, creates an ever increasing requirement to safeguard the landscape and its wildlife. This must be accentuated by the small area of the A.N.O.B. Despite its 25 sq. miles in size, it is the smallest area of any mainland A.N.O.B. As an outsider looking in, so to speak, the balance appears to be about right. It is certainly one of the county's treasures and rightly so. The visitor centres carry a large range of leaflets on different aspects of the Chase, many free and a few available for a few pence each. All are rec-ommended. All centres have a café/toilets etc. Not mentioned above is a fifth Visitor Centre, which also serves the Chase, but has a larger educational function it is own right. This is Shugborough Hall at the northern tip of the Chase.

Cannock Chase has a large Com-monwealth War Cemetery and nearby, a German War Cemetery. Nearly 300 German personnel are buried here.

Shugborough

Situated to the east of Stafford this large country house, better known as the home of the late Patrick Lichfield (5th Earl of Lichfield), is now owned by the

National Trust, but leased by Staffordshire County Council. Pevsner states that 'for picturesque grounds and garden furnishings, few houses in England can compete with Shugborough. The approach from the Milford Lodges is an experience which will never be forgotten'. In fact Pevsner goes on to say that for buildings in parks 'Staffordshire may well be the richest county in England'. In addition to Shugborough, there are ornamental buildings in quite a few parks including Weston Park and Chillington, which are open to the public, Sandon (open only to groups of visitors) and others which are not open, such as Ingestre.

It is a pity that this is not pointed out on the information boards at the side of the drive which you pass on the way in. Pevsner has in mind (one assumes) the view towards the tower on the left, close to the river – the Lanthorn (Lantern) of Demoshenes – and the Triumphal Arch above on the right, both of which are early 1760s. The former, together with the Tower of the Winds, which is between The Farm and the Mansion, are the earliest neo-Grecian buildings in England. The Tower of the Winds is also close to the drive and Pevsner presumably had this in mind too.

Other monuments are The Ruin, by the River Sow and visible from the house; the Doric Temple; Shepherds Monument and the lovely Chinese House and adjacent Chinese Bridge. The Chinese House dates from 1747 and is one of the earliest oriental garden buildings in the country. Look out for other monuments additional to those referred to.

There is much to see and do here. Having parked your car (there is a fee),

the Ticket Office leads you to the Walled Garden of 1805 and then The Farm of the same date. You can walk or catch a free bus between the two (and also the House). Both of these are run by the County Council and your car parking fee is redeemable against the cost of your visit to the Servants Quarters beyond, now housing the County Museum. (National Trust members enter the house free with the same car park fee redeemed against the Museum entrance fee).

The Farm is run as it would have been in olden days and the farmhouse is arranged accordingly, with a dairy making butter and cheese and the kitchen still making bread from its bread oven. Outside the watermill still operates, grinding flour with its waterwheel still providing the power for the grindstones. Look out for the Staffordshire-style wagon in one of the out-buildings. It is very rare, possibly one of only two survivors, the other being in the Les Oaks' collection at Cheadle.

Moving on to the Servants' Quarters, this is a block adjacent to the house. Here, the rooms are furnished as they would have been in days gone by and other rooms laid out with items from the County Museum collection. It is an impressive layout, including the carriage collection formerly owned by the Earl of Shrewsbury. Your tour includes the kitchen, scullery, servants' hall etc. There is a lot to see here, so allocate a good hour or more.

You emerge from the museum adjacent to the entrance front of the house; a remarkable facade comprising the results of various building periods and all harmonious. The garden front at the rear doesn't appear to be lacking too much, but Palliser in '*The Staffordshire Landscape*' describes it as being ugly, probably because of the State Rooms projecting in a pronounced bow in the middle of the front.

The current house dates from 1693 with extensions in 1748 and even more alterations in the 1760s when Stuart worked here, followed by Samuel Wyatt thirty years later on a scheme which lasted until 1806. It is the home of the Anson family who acquired it in 1624 and remain to this day. The oldest son of each generation bears the name Thomas and the Earldom of Lichfield was bestowed in 1831. Much of the house remains in use by the family, but there is much to see before moving on to the grounds between the house and the River Sow.

Poignantly, there are reminders of Patrick Lichfield and his photography on your tour of the house. It is pleasant to see these to recall a much missed man and cousin of H.M. The Queen. When you leave here, if you travel east you are only a couple of miles or so from the Wolseley Centre, the HQ of the Staffordshire Wildlife Trust. They are just beyond the junction with the A51.

Places to Visit

Stafford Castle

Newport Road ST16 1DJ
☎ 01785 257698
www.staffordbc.gov.uk.uk/heritage
Open: Apr–Oct daily except Mon 10am-5pm. Winter Sat & Sun 10am-4pm. Bank Holidays 10am-5pm
Ⓟ ♿ (to Visitor Centre and path to Castle remains) 🚻 (free) ☂

Staffordshire County Showground

Weston Road Stafford ST18 0BD
☎ 01785 258060
www.staffscountyshowground.co.uk
County Show–end of May
There is a regular monthly programme of shows and fairs

The Ancient High House

Greengate Street, ST16 2JA
☎ 01785 619131
www.staffordbc.gov.uk/heritageevents
Open: Tues-Sat, 10am-4pm
♿ (but limited) 🚻 (free) ☂

Izaak Walton Cottage

Worston Lane
Shallowford, ST15 0PA
☎ 01785 760278
www.staffordbc.gov.uk/heritage
Open: May–Aug, Sat & Sun, 1pm-5pm
Ⓟ ♿ 🚻 (free)

Places to Visit

Go Ape!

Birches Valley Forest Centre
Cannock Forest
Ladyhill
Rugeley. WS15 2UQ
Book ahead (essential) on goape.co.uk
or call
☎ 0845 094 8756
Minimum age 10 years.
Open: Late May–end-Oct and some
later weekends
℗ ⋔ (concession 10-17 years)

Visitor Centres, Cannock Chase Area

There are waymarked trails at all of
these sites, except the Museum.

Birches Valley Forest Centre

(Forestry Enterprise)
Lady Hill
Birches Valley
Rugeley WS15 2UQ
☎ 01889 586593
www.forestry.gov.uk/england
Open: Shop 11am-3.30pm, site open
daylight hours.
Cycle hire/racks, picnic area, cafe, gift
shop.
℗ ⋔ (free) ⌇

Cannock Chase Visitor Centre

(Staffordshire County Council)
Marquis Drive
Hednesford WS12 4PW
☎ 01543 871773
www.staffordshire.gov.uk

Open: Cafe/Visitor Centre Apr–Sep,
daily 10am-5.30pm; reduced hours in
winter.
Cycle hire, picnic area, cafe, gift shop.
℗ ⋔ free ⌇

Museum of Cannock Chase

(Cannock Chase Council)
☎ 01543 877666
www.cannockchasedc.gov.uk/museum
Open: Easter–end-Sep, daily 11am-
5pm (4pm winter)
℗ ⋔ (free; charge for guided tours) ⌇

Shugborough Estate

Milford
Stafford ST17 0XB
☎ 01889 881388
www.shugborough.org.uk
Open: Mid March–late Oct, daily 11am-
5pm
℗ ⋔ (family ticket) ⌇
Step back into history with real historic
working environments, plus the Hall
tour.

Wolseley Bridge

nr Little Haywood, Stafford, ST17 0WT
☎ 01889 880100
www.staffs-wildlife.org.uk
Open daily 9am-5pm (Mon-Fri); 11am-
5pm Sat-Sun.
℗ ⋔ ⌇
26 ac (10h) of habitats, cafe, gift shop.

5. The Lower Dove and West to Blithfield Reservoir

This chapter covers the valley of the River Dove between Denstone and Sudbury and the area west of Uttoxeter and down to Abbots Bromley and Blithfield Reservoir.

The chapter starts at **Cheadle** in the north. Here is situated **St. Giles** Roman Catholic Church (the COE is also dedicated to St. Giles). It was built in the 1840s, a happy partnership between the Earl of Shrewsbury and his architect A.W.N. Pugin. Constructed in Gothic Revival style, it is often noted as the best ecclesiastical work of that style anywhere. Pugin referred to it as 'Cheadle, perfect Cheadle'.

There was apparently no initial intention to paint it internally, but the Earl got the idea in Paris and came back enthused. It knocks you back a little at first, but everything here is of such high quality, it does grow on you somewhat.

A visit is certainly recommended and also that you allow sufficient time

Ramblers' Retreat, Dimmingsdale, near Alton

to look around thoroughly. It deserves nothing less. Here is architecture expressing the Glory of God. Built by a man at the height of his profession, with the enthusiastic encouragement of his patron, it does so perfectly; just as Pugin believed it should be.

This section of the Dove Valley was used for the Uttoxeter Canal section of the Caldon until January 1847, when

Sudbury Hall

a lot of the canal bed was used for the new North Staffordshire Railway track and so it remained until Dr. Beating's Report condemned the railway below Okemoor to history. Industrial archaeologists will not find too much of the railway line of interest now, but there is an interesting section of the canal remaining at **Crumpwood Weir**, just north of Denstone and which may be reached on foot. Here the canal crossed the River Churnet behind a stone weir (now called Crumpwood Weir). The horses paddled through the river which flows in a shallow form over the weir. It is worth going to see. It is wide enough to ensure horses did not fall off and can be accessed along the lane running up the east side of the river from near Denstone Bridge. Whilst in the area, Denstone church is also worth visiting.

It is one of the county's five Gothic Revival Churches mentioned on p.13. Down river is **Rocester**, now dominated by the JCB Excavator works set in parkland and with two large lakes. These attract a lot of waterfowl and also have a number of ornamental species including black swans. There was a Roman fort here and later, a Augustinian Priory, but there is very little to see of either.

The road westwards to Hollington from Rocester rises away from the valley and after a few miles there is a right turn to Great Gate. This takes you to **Croxden Abbey**, one of three Cistercian Abbeys in the county and the only one of the three to have substantial remains. They rise to almost roof height at the west end of the nave of the abbey church and the south wall of the south transept are lower but still substantial, although the east end has gone completely and even has the road crossing the site. They date from the late 12th - late 13th century. Now in the care of English Heritage, it is worth a visit and the interpretation boards are, as usual, useful and enable one to appreciate how things used to appear here.

The good quality stone of the area not only gave good service here at Croxden, but still provides building stone to this day at nearby Hollington which provided the stone for Coventry Cathedral in 1962.

Below Rocester, the road runs down the old railway line to **Uttoxeter**. The town is one of only a handful where the local authority owns a racecourse, which today is the main visitor attraction. Dr. Johnson's father had a bookstall here on market day. As an old man, Dr. Johnson stood here in the rain with his hat off to pay penitence for refusing to help out on the stall as a lad. The event is celebrated with a monument in the town centre. The pedestrianised main street is attractive and I have it on good authority that the town centre toilets are second to none!

Uttoxeter has a Heritage Centre in Carter Street. It is housed in a 17th Century timber framed building. There are displays on the history of the town and it has a courtyard garden to relax in.

It is only a matter of minutes from here on the A50 to **Sudbury**, which should not be missed. It sits on the Derbyshire bank of the River Dove, but it of sufficient interest to include a mention here.

The hall of Elizabethan and Jacobean

style dates from the 17th Century. It has recently featured in *Pride and Prejudice* and *Jane Eyre*.

It was the home of the Vernon family, who still live nearby. However, they gave the hall to the National Trust. It is a large house and is very impressive when viewed from the road through the village. It is truly a magnificent house with richly decorated interiors and carving by Grinling Gibbons. After looking around the main rooms, you can discover what life was like 'below stairs' in the 1930s kitchen. The garden is relatively small, being given over to lawns which stretch down to a lake at the rear.

The **National Trust Museum of Childhood** is housed here and has had a £2.2m redevelopment recently. It is a must for younger visitors. (The village itself is small but has a good inn: The Vernon Arms). The kids can climb 'chimnies', enjoy the experience of a Victorian schoolroom and explore eight galleries which include activities for the whole family. Queen Adelaide lived here as a widow for a while, but found the house too cold in winter. She was the wife of William IV.

To the west of Uttoxeter, the Stafford road leads to Weston, past the remains of **Chartley Castle** on the right. They are clearly visible from the road, but are not accessible to the public. Three towers remain to a reasonable height. They were originally five of them, 40 feet in diameter and with walls 12 feet thick. It was built in 1220. Mary Queen of Scots was taken from here to Fotheringay Castle, Northants, for her trial prior to execution.

To be precise, she was housed at the adjacent Chartley Hall, as the castle has become a ruin. The hall was destroyed by fire in 1781 and the current hall is of mid-19th century date. It is not open to the public.

At **Weston**, on the west side of the village and by the Stafford road is Jacobean Weston Hall, now a conference centre, restaurant and guest house of some standing. Beyond, after a couple of miles is the County Showground and home of the County Show.

On reaching the A51 at Weston, a right turn soon brings you to Sandon. There isn't much to detain you here unless the Hall, home of Lord Harrowby, is open but you have to be in a prebooked party to gain access.

To the south of the A518, Uttoxeter to Stafford road, is **Abbots Bromley** and Blithfield Reservoir. The road to the village is just out of Uttoxeter, as you climb up the road out of the town. Abbots Bromley is now a quiet village with a large private school. It is a pretty village and the Butter Cross and adjacent timber framed Goat's Head Inn make a pleasant scene.

The annual Horn Dance here is, like many truly old English customs, something which has been held 'since the memory of man runneth not to the contrary!' Whether it's centuries or millennia isn't known and could be the latter. The ceremony takes up a whole day with a lot of dancing with carved deer heads and ancient deer antlers attached (otherwise kept in the church). Maid Marion is in attendance, a reminder of the tradition that Robin Hood was Lord of the Manor at Yoxall (on the A515 a little to the east) and supposedly married Maid Marion at Tutbury.

Nearby, **Blithfield Reservoir** is, at first glance, a depressing sheet of water, but has its importance. It was constructed in 1952 and covers 790 acres/320 ha. A notice board advises that it ranks amongst the nation's most significant waters for wildfowl and immigrant waders. Bird watchers, anglers and sailors can learn more on ℅ 01283 840283. The large country house on the west side is Blithfield Hall, home of the Bagot family for many generations (it is not open to the public). The B-road across the reservoir soon brings you to the A51 and a left turn brings you to a roundabout and the Wolseley Centre, home of the Staffordshire Wildlife Trust (see p.8).

A mile east of Weston on the A518 Stafford–Uttoxeter road, east of the A51 is **Amerton Farm and Craft Centre**. There are a lot of attractions here and there is no general admission charge. Tuesday is Senior Citizen day and Friday is Toddlers Discount day (during Staffordshire school term time). There are a lot of shops, craft workshops; balloon flights; British Wildlife Rescue Centre; farmhouse bed and breakfast and much more.

Places to Visit

Amerton Farm & Craft Centre

Stoweby Chartley, Stafford, ST18 0LA
☎ 01889 270294
www.amertonfarm.co.uk
Heart of England Tourism Award for Visitor Attraction of the Year 2005
Open daily 9am - 5.30pm Easter - Christmas; 5pm Christmas - Easter. Not open 25-6 December and 1ˢᵗ January.
Ⓟ ⋔ (free) ☂

Croxden Abbey

Great Gate Nr. Rocester
Open daily 10am-5pm
Ⓟ ⋔ ☂

Museum of Childhood (N.T.)

Sudbury Hall, Sudbury
Open March–end-October, 11am-5pm Wed-Sun (and Mon-Tues August and 1ˢᵗ week in September). Also open in December, 10.30 - 3.30pm, Sat - Sun.
Ⓟ ♿ (but restricted in hall) ⋔ ☂

Sudbury Hall (N.T.)

Sudbury, Nr. Ashbourne, DE6 5HT
☎ 01283 585305
Hall open Mar–end-Oct 1pm-5pm, Wed-Sun

Uttoxeter Heritage Centre

34-36 Carter Street, ST14 8EU
☎ 01889 567176
Open Tues–Sat 10am-4pm
♿ ⋔ (free)

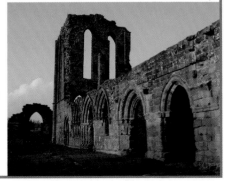

Croxdon Abbey

National Memorial Arboretum, Alrewas

Lichfield lies in the Vale of the River Trent, essentially low lying river gravels yielding sand and gravel for the building industry from under good agricultural land.

This chapter covers the area sloping down to the River Trent with Lichfield, Tamworth and Burton-on-Trent the main communities. Situated adjacent to the A38 and yet another of those sand pits is the **National Memorial Arboretum** at Alrewas. Here the nation honours its military who have paid the ultimate price of service to Crown, Country and pals since 1945. There are now over 150 major memorials.

It is a quiet, moving, even sobering place. You walk on paths amid 50,000 trees slowly gaining in height. You rub shoulders with heroes standing in quiet contemplation; memories still fresh of lives given in one conflict after another. The central feature, the Armed Forces Memorial, is the memorial where all those who have died since 1945 have their names carved in the stone panels. Here is a bronze wreath, aligned to the sun in such a way that if it shines at 11am on the 11th day of the 11th month it lightens on the wreath.

It is an unforgettable experience and that is how it should be. Surprisingly perhaps there are lots of visitors and that too is how it should be. From here it is only a few minutes on the A38 to Lichfield, but first a diversion up the A515 towards Sudbury is recommended.

Leaving the National Memorial and turning right, the road crosses the A38 and heads for **Kings Bromley**. A right turn here on the A515 leads to Yoxall and then Newchurch. At the crossroads by the church, there are places of visit to the left and right. The turn left goes down to **Hoar Cross** with its village pub on a crossroads. The road ahead climbs up a hill to Hoar Cross Hall on the left.

The Hall was the home of the Meynell Ingram family. The house is in Elizabethan-style, dating from the early 1870s. Hugo Meynell Ingram had married Emily Wood, daughter of the 1st Viscount Halifax, in 1863. The hall is similar to Temple Newsam, near Leeds, the Meynell Ingram's principal home. In 1871 two years after succeeding his father, Hugo died following a hunting accident. Emily succeeded to her husband's wealth, making her one of the richest women of independent means

in the country. When she died in 1904 her annual income was c. £168,000. The hall stood within an estate of 8,800 acres.

Today the hall is a very high quality hotel, with much investment in the Eden Day Spa Centre adjoining. Here you can come and be pampered in style, within a lovely house and gardens. It is certainly something special. However many guests probably leave without realising that there is a real treasure of a church next door. In fact it is in the best piece of ecclesiastical architecture by G.F. Bodley in the Gothic Revival style. Staffordshire is fortunate to have the best church architecture of no less than five architects in this style (see p.13).

Following the death of her husband, Emily built this church in her husband's memory and could afford not to be too concerned at what it cost her. Her memorial is now one of Staffordshire's treasures and well worth a visit. The memory of Hugo also lives on with the Meynell Hunt, with which Prince Charles used to ride until the change in legislation.

Also worth a visit if the calendar permits, is **Yoxall Lodge Farm**, by turning east at Newchurch. A couple of miles or so brings one to the farm drive on the right. The former country seat here has been demolished, but its former estate includes some very ancient woodlands. Some of these are carpeted in spring by **bluebells** - millions of them, or at least that is the lasting impression.

For a few weeks each year, woodland trails convey visitors who come to stand and marvel at yet another hidden secret of this county. The National Forest Centre at Moira to the south east (beyond Burton-on-Trent) highlights two other areas where bluebells can be seen en masse. To see great swathes of the flowers moving in the wind and inhale the pleasing scent is to see and experience rural England at its best.

The A515 continues north towards Draycott in the Clay and Sudbury. Just prior to descending the escarpment to Draycott, a right turn leads down country lanes to **Hanbury**. Here is a huge crater in the fields and it marks the largest man-made, non-nuclear explosion ever. An underground bomb store blew up during World War II. Seismologists recorded it in Moscow and over 70 people lost their lives in the disaster. A few years ago there was a proposal to turn the crater into a rubbish dump; unbelievable municipal insensitivity quickly being dropped.

The A515 leaves Draycott and soon crosses the River Dove and leaves the county. Immediately ahead is Sudbury with its lovely hall, village and Museum of Childhood (see p.69).

Lichfield

Back at the A38, Lichfield beckons.

Lichfield has been described as the best Georgian town in the county and indeed it must be. Its best street being Bove Street. It owes its reputation by chance and we are the better for it. Both Newcastle and Lichfield shunned industrial development, although the former saw plenty of industry on its doorstep, with coal mines, forges and marl working to the north and west. Lichfield kept the industry and the railway at bay. The canal came only to about a mile away to the south, delivering coal and other cargoes. It is not just the lack of industry that resulted in the proud accolade: the city also managed to resist the temptation to rebuild the town centre in more recent times. The result is a harmonious blend of properties stretching away from its magnificent cathedral.

The town became a cultural centre; Samuel Johnson was born here, Erasmus Darwin lived here. Today, it must be the **cathedral** that it its finest treasure. It owes its foundation to Saxon St. Chad, but the current structure is basically medieval.

It is the only cathedral in the country where three spires representing the blessed Trinity have survived – two at the west end and one above a crossing tower, where the nave, chancel and transepts meet. The latter spire collapsed during the Civil War bombardment, falling on the choir, but fortunately it was rebuilt. Not only is the west front one of the most impressive in the country but the building has two large pools nearby – Minster Pool and Stowe Pool. Viewed across either of these sheets of water, the cathedral presents an impressive and memorable sight, adding a sense of grandeur denied many other cathedrals. Not only did the Georgian properties survive, so did the pools, avoiding car parks and the temptation of other developments.

Having taking in the view from either (or both) of these two pools, one can hardly fail to marvel at the west front with its rows of statuary and intricate carving. However, these are of not great age – they are of late Victo-

Above and inset: Lichfield Cathedral

Opposite page top left: The sleeping children, Lichfield Cathedral; top right: Dr Johnson, Lichfield market place; bottom: The Close, Lichfield Cathedral

rian provenance. That hardly seems to matter. If the purists are offended, so be it. The cathedral is definitely enhanced by their presence and perhaps that is enough. If your curiosity stretches to wondering if any of the statues are original survivors, there is a good one near to the south porch. It is 17th century and the face is now badly eroded. It is of Charles II and commemorates his gift of money and timber for the restoration of the cathedral. It had suffered badly from Cromwell's batteries, which had brought down the crossing tower spire. If you look carefully, you will see that it is of different stone to the other spires.

As one might expect from a building like this, the interior does not disappoint. Perhaps the highlight from the perspective of its monuments is Sir Francis Chantrey's carving of the two Robinson children, two young girls locked in a perpetual, final embrace. It is often claimed to be Chantrey's finest work and its intimate, closely worked detail is a joy to see, let alone the intricate detail of the rood screen, the Minton tiles in the choir stalls and so on. At certain times you can also ascend the crossing tower for magnificent views of the city.

This is of course a House of God, which welcomes all persuasions to a full programme of cultural events and there cannot be another attraction in the county which opens its doors at 7.30 in the morning. This huge building accommodates these events, the curious visitor, those seeking quiet reflection or prayer, all at the same time; in harmony and with shared reverence for such a wonderful building in the sight of God.

Surrounding the cathedral is The Close, a grouping of fine buildings, now mainly houses and apartments. On the north side is the Deanery and next to it the former Bishop's Palace, now a school, the Bishop living at a second palace near Eccleshall. Facing the west front of the cathedral on the corner of the street is a timber framed building with an entry, which gives access to the Erasmus Darwin Museum. Darwin, the grandfather of Charles Darwin, lived in Lichfield between 1756-81. To get to it, you wander through a herb garden, resplendent in Spring when in flower and with a lovely scent at all times. There is a tablet to him on the south side of the cathedral's chancel.

Facing the Market Place is the **Samuel Johnson birthplace museum**. Here you can learn more about the great man and his companion and biographer, James Boswell. Both knew Ashbourne well, which also has a fine Georgian Street which both men would recognise today. They were frequent visitors to Dr. Taylor who lived in that street (Church Street) at The Mansion. It is situated opposite the Old Grammar School. Johnson walked to Ashbourne from Lichfield for an interview for the position of the Assistant Master. Having failed to secure the position he had to walk back again, presumably to this house.

Johnson was apparently to be rejected by Ashbourne a second time, for he sought the hand of Dr. Taylor's daughter, but was declined. Taylor's home is in Church Street, which turns into St. John Street where the last house on the right carries a plaque recording that Erasmus Darwin's three daughters ran a school at the premises.

The **Lichfield Heritage Centre** is also in the Market Place and has displays on The Lichfield Story, similar to Tamworth Castle's equivalent on that town; an exhibition of Staffordshire Millennium Embroideries and The Treasury, showing silver plate, chalices of the city, churches and Staffordshire Regiment. There are two audio-visual presentations, covering the Civil War and the history of Lichfield and interactive activity for children.

Dominating the Market Place is a statue of Johnson, erected in 1838 and facing his birthplace. He sits in contemplation amid frenetic trading of stall holders on market days, no doubt not so very different from the activities he would have known prior to his death in 1784.

Tamworth

Tamworth is the county's oldest town, existing by the end of the 8th century. It became the capital of Mercia and Offa (best remembered for his Dyke) had his palace here during that century. It may have later been on the boundary between the Danelaw and Saxon England. The town was divided between Staffordshire and Warwickshire until 1890 and the former part is where the Danish street names still exist, e.g. Ellergate, Aldergate etc. The boundary ran along Gumpegate, up Church Street and along Holloway to Lady Bridge.

The town was sacked by the Danes in 874 and fortified in 913. The town had a royal mint and along with Stafford was the only town recorded before 1086, the date of the Domesday Book. The town was fortified by Ethelfleda (King Alfred's daughter) following the defeat of the Danes near Wednesfield, cementing Saxon domination of the area. A little later the Danes united with the Mercians following the marriage in Tamworth of King Athelstan's (King of Wessex and King of England 926 - 939) sister Editha to the Danish king Sihtric in 926 and the **ancient church** is dedicated to her. It is the only church in the county (other than Ilam) to exhibit Saxon architecture. When she died (at Tamworth), the Mercians declared allegiance to her brother Edward and it has been suggested that the county of Stafford may have come into existence at about that time ('*The Staffordshire Landscape*', D. Palliser).

It was the Normans who raised the motte and bailey **castle** later replacing the wooden defences with stone in the late 12th century. Much of the interior dates from Jacobean times with much of the inner space being built on, but the Great Hall is much older. There are some 15 rooms open to the public. Owned by the town, it is cared for by Friends of the Castle who make a good job of it too. The various periods of history are portrayed in its rooms. Some are old and relatively simply furnished, others later and more elegant. Additionally there is the 'Tamworth Story' portraying the history of the town and some of its sons, notably Robert Peel, who as Home Secretary founded the Metropolitan Police.

The castle achieved 4th place in the UK TV History poll (the only castle to feature in the top ten of Britain's historic sites) and was also winner of the Sandford Award for Education. Tamworth Castle represents a unique interpretation of life in a small castle, particularly its use as a fortified residence. It also represents good value for your admission fee; both for adults and children.

On the north side of the castle is Market Street, the main shopping street, dominated by the Town Hall of 1701. It was paid for by Thomas Guy who is better known for giving his name to Guy's Hospital in London. It is open on the ground floor with its arches supported on Tuscan columns. Here market traders have sold their wares for centuries. In front of the building is a bronze statue of Sir Robert Peel, the town's MP from 1830 to 1850. Look out also for the Moat House of 1572 and the Manor House, both in Lichfield Street. Pevsner, however, reserves his best praise for the town's best house to Bole Hall in Amington Road, out to the south east of the town.

If you are looking for something more recent and, subject to taste, something more dynamic, try the Snowdome, a discreet distance from the castle but visible from it. Real snow and ice offer sporting activity all the year round; lots of fun too by all accounts.

Better known for a fun day out is **Drayton Manor Park**. The elegant former country house has gone but the Park hosts a nationally known and revered amusement park, incorporating thrilling rides and voted best UK value destination. It also incorporates *Thomas Land* based upon Thomas the Tank Engine. The park is just outside the south west side of Tamworth.

A more tranquil experience than the thrill rides are to be found at the **Middleton Equestrian Centre** and

Twycross Zoo, set in another parkland across the border in nearby Warwickshire at Atherstone. Here is one of the western world's top collection of primate species and home to about 1,000 animals. Middleton Hall is also open to the public. A Grade II listed house, it is also a site of special scientific interest and former home of two British naturalists - Francis Willughby and John Ray. Part of the hall is a 16th century jettied building.

Finally if you were thinking that there was another connection with Tamworth, you could be correct. Remember the Tamworth Two, the escapees who avoided capture for a week a decade ago? Not prisoners who hogged the limelight and captured the nation's attention and admiration, but two pigs. The Tamworth pig is the domestic species closest to the wild boar apparently. These two however ended celebrity status following capture with not the butcher's block but pensioned off to a long life in a green field, having been saved by a national newspaper. Who says no good comes from reading newspapers?

Just to the north of Burton-on-Trent is **Tutbury** with its ancient castle and priory. Today the remains of the castle and the priory church are a direct link with the town's ancient past. Less well known is that it was the penultimate place for the final bull running festival held in England (the last place being Stamford in Lincolnshire). The Duke of Devonshire paid for the bull (£2) and once a year Staffordshire had its own Pamplona. However a meeting finally held in Ashbourne bought about its demise in the 1770s.

Above left: Thomas Land, Drayton Manor Park; above right: Tamworth with the statue of Sir Robert Peel and Guy's Town Hall behind

Above: Tutbury Castle

Tutbury was a crossing of the River Dove, with a highway heading for Ashbourne, the original southern gateway to the Peak. Situated close to the crossing are the remains of its castle. Of Norman foundation, it was refurbished, extended etc over the centuries. It came to the Duchy of Lancaster and has belonged to the monarch since 1399 when the Duke of Lancaster ascended to the throne as Henry IV.

He came here as did James I and Charles I. Mary, Queen of Scots, was a prisoner here under her charge, William Cavendish, in 1569-70 and again in 1585. The Cavendish family (later Earls/Dukes of Devonshire) were the tenants of the Duchy.

Following the Civil War, Cromwell's troops slighted the castle and much of it was destroyed. Nevertheless, enough survives to give a good idea of what it was like.

Nearby is the priory church, now the parish church. It survived the dissolution of the monasteries by becoming the town church. It has a glorious west front and is one of the county's treasures. A similar situation happened in Burton-on-Trent where there was an impressive abbey church. It survived long enough for it to be drawn reasonably carefully. However it was demolished to make way for the current Georgian church in 1719. With the closure of the former Bass Museum in 2008 by its new owners - Coors

- it is Tutbury which has the interest for visitors. Indeed, Palliser describes Tutbury Priory (essentially the nave of the latter's church) as the grandest and most unspoilt Norman church in the county.

Travelling from Burton-on-Trent on the A444 towards Junction 11 on the M42, in Overseal there is a left turn to **Conkers**, the 120 acre/48 ha Visitor Centre of the National Forest. The logo on the brown directional roadsigns is of a stylised merry-go-round. Conkers has much to offer young people and their parents, with the education of all about the environment being a subtle theme behind the attractions. There are also trails to explore and details of heritage attractions in the area. There is plenty for the adventurous too; in fact enough to keep everyone going for ages!

There is a lot to see and do here, hence an adjacent Camping and Caravanning Club park and also a modern, purpose-built youth hostel especially catering for families and groups (for information and bookings ring the YHA Contact Centre on ☎ 01629 592700).

The National Forest Visitor Guide is commendable as what a major attraction visitor guide ought to be. Much of it of course is outside Staffordshire but it includes every conceivable item of interest for visitors for quite a distance away from Conkers, covering attractions, activities and accommodation. It's also free.

Places to Visit

Erasmus Darwin House

Beacon Street, WS13 7AD
☎ 01543 306260
enquiries@erasmusdarwin.org
Open: Thurs-Sun, noon-5pm
(last admission 4.15pm)
& ♯♯♯ (family ticket) ☞

Lichfield Cathedral

Chapter Office
19A The Close, WS13 7LD
☎ 01543 306100
www.lichfield-cathedral.org
Open: Daily 7.30-6.15pm

Lichfield Garrick (Theatre)

Castle Dyke, WS13 6HR
☎ 01543 412121 (box office)

Lichfield Heritage Centre

Market Square, WS13 6LG
☎ 01543 256611
Open: Daily 9.30am-5pm, Sun 10am-
4pm
& ♯♯♯ (family ticket) ☞

Lichfield Market Days - Tues, Fri, Sat
Farmers Market - First Thurs of month
(except Jan), 9am - 3pm
Markets are held in Market Square

Samuel Johnson Birthplace Museum

Breadmarket Street, WS13 6LG
☎ 01543 264972
www.samueljohnsonbirthplace.org
Open: Daily, Apr–Sept 10.30-4.30pm;
Oct–Dec 11am-5.30pm; Jan–Mar noon-
4.30pm, closed Christmas and 1st Jan
& ♯♯♯ (free) ☞

Tourist Information Centre

Lichfield Garrick

Castle Dyke, WS13 6HR
☎ 01543 412112
www.visitlichfield.com

National Memorial Arboretum

Croxall Road
Alrewas
Staffs, DE13 7AR
☎ 01283 792333
Open: Daily 9am-5pm
Ⓟ & ♯♯♯ (free) ☞

Staffordshire Regiment Museum

Whittington Barracks
☎ 01543 434390
Open: Mon–Fri 10am-4.30pm plus
weekends Apr–Oct and BH Mon.
Closed Christmas and New Year period
Ⓟ & ♯♯♯ ☞

Tamworth Castle

The Holloway
Ladybank, B79 7NA
☎ 01827 709629
www.tamworthcastle.co.uk
Open: Apr–Sept, Tues-Sun, noon-5.15pm,
winter, Sat & Sun noon-5.15pm
* (nearby car parks)/+/$ (family ticket)/÷
(in part)

Conkers

Rawdon Road
Moira, DE12 6GA
☎ 01283 216633
www.visitconkers.com

7. The South West

You would be hard pressed to suggest that this area is well known to visitors to the county. The comparison with the north-east of the county could not be greater from that point of view. This is a shame, for the area has a lot to offer.

It consists, for the purposes of this book, of the area south west of Stafford, stretching to the Shropshire border - roughly the area west of the M6 and an area north of the M54 plus a strange extension south of the M54. It is barely five or six miles wide and about fifteen miles long. When Dudley and Wolverhampton ceded from the county, the remaining area west of Dudley - (the former Snelsdon Rural District Council) stayed within Staffordshire and it extended down to Kinver and remains so.

However the area is worth a visit; the scenery is not too special, but some of its attractions most certainly are special. Moreover, there are other places worth

Left: Halfpenny Green Vineyard

Opposite page: Weston Park, Weston-Under-Lizard

Above: Kinver Edge Rock Houses and Country Park; below: Mosley Old Hall (N.T.) north of Wolverhampton

considering just beyond the county boundary, such as the RAF Museum at Cosford and Bridgnorth to the west. Approaching Kinver from junction 3 of the M5 you pass through undulating countryside which is largely well wooded. This landscape continues into Staffordshire and there are numerous walks available in a woodland setting north of Kinver.

However the main attraction in the Kinver area is Kinver Edge and the **Holy Austin Rock Cottages** on the Edge and now cared for by the National Trust. The Edge is an escarpment of sandstone with the scarp to the south affording extensive views to the south and west into Worcestershire and Shropshire. The Edge has as Iron Age Fort, but it is the Rock Houses at Holy Austin Rock (he was apparently a monk) which is well worth going to see. Occupied until 1965 as a café, residential occupation ended in the 1950s, the home of some of England's last cave dwellers. Whole houses with several rooms were excavated by hand out of the rock and some have now been restored. They are surprisingly of good size, with interconnecting passages between rooms. Although simply furnished, they were warm in winter and cool in summer; the parlour still has an open fire and cooking range. The contrast between this humble home and the National Trust's home at Wightwick Manor to the north could not be greater. The country's last cave dweller may well have been Doug Moller who lived at Rock Cottage on The Roaches, north of Leek, still in Staffordshire. Doug lived there certainly into the late 1980s and possibly later.

If you can read a map, the network of minor lanes to the north head in the direction of Wightwick, but there area a couple of diversions on the way. Just north of the Wolverhampton Airport at **Halfpenny Green** is a **Vineyard and Craft Centre**. It comes as a surprise, for it's a fairly busy place, reflecting its various attractions. Road signs to 'Vineyard' assist navigation and the latter, covering 25 acres/10 ha is clearly an unusual attraction with tasting, and shop sales at a discount. There is a traditional English tearoom and restaurant and a relaxing coffee lounge. Outside are several craft workshops making or processing various items including aromatherapy oils, herbs and olives. Admission is free and its rural location gives you a good opportunity to explore this little bit of Staffordshire.

To the north east is Wombourne and just to the north on the Staffordshire-Worcestershire Canal are the three-tier **Bratch locks**, again reasonably well signposted. A small car park exists and if you have bought your own lunch, it's a good place to stop for a while and try and work out the various water courses augmenting water supplies to the canal as boats move up and down.

Just to the north is the A454 and just inside the boundary of Wolverhampton is the National Trust direction sign for **Wightwick Manor**. It was the home of Geoffrey Mander, of Mander's Paints. The front facing the South Terrace is very impressive but it is the contents which make this large house important.

The National Trust is particularly fortunate here for the house has a nationally recognised collection of William Morris furnishings, fabrics, wallpapers and stained glass proudly stated as such in the Trust's literature. There are works by followers of the Arts and Crafts Movement and a growing collection of Pre-Raphaelite art, including paintings by Burne-Jones, Millais and Rossetti. Moreover, the garden extends the exuberance of colour seen in the house, through the growing season.

Despite the impressive artwork collection, the architectural style is impressive too. The promise of 'more within' extended by the house's appearance from the South Terrace does not disappoint and the medieval-style Great Parlour, looking like a 15th Century Great Hall (it is actually mid-19th century) has been cleverly done.

Another National Trust property in the area, just south of the M54 and halfway between junctions 1 and 2 is **Moseley Old Hall**. Charles II's generosity to Lichfield Cathedral (see chapter 6) was no doubt coloured by memories of another earlier occasion when he took refuge at this house. Here he hid after his defeat at the Battle of Worcester in 1651. This Elizabethan house, altered in the 19th century, still retains the bed used by the king and the full story is covered by the guided tour and in an exhibition in former farm buildings. An interest is the Knot Garden which was created here in 1962 and is a copy of the garden of 1640 at Darfield Rectory, near Barnsley. It compliments the house rather well. There is a well stocked orchard, including the appropriate Black Worcester pear. This is a 17th century variety and a good preserve pear, according to one of the many helpful volunteers at this pleasant place. There is a programme of events from March to October and children's activities every Tuesday (2pm - 4pm) during August.

Just inside the western boundary of the county is **Weston Park**, one of the county's finest houses, dating from 1671. It is a large three storey house, a very early attempt at classical style architecture. Its collection is large and of the first order, from furniture, tapestries to old master paintings. Its facilities for younger visitors are comprehensive and for older visitors, there are also Public Events throughout the year.

The park and gardens were set out by Lancelot 'Capability' Brown and his work survives intact. It includes many ornamental buildings and the finest is The Temple of Diana by James Payne. As you wander around the park - whether its here, Shugborough or at Chillington - it's worth putting them into context. They represent one of the county's major contributions to Georgian England as Palliser reminds us in his '*The Staffordshire Landscape*'.

Chillington Hall, as noted above, is another house with a garden by 'Capability' Brown - so called because he advised clients that their land had 'capabilities'. It is situated at Codsall Wood, south east of Weston Park and just south of the M54. Brown obviously meant what he said here for his lake is one of the largest that he constructed and was an immediate success, dating from 1761.

The house only offers limited opening times so check before you set off. It is between junctions 2 and 3 of the M54.

Just to the west of Chillington Hall is a collection of a different nature: **RAF Cosford Museum**. It is just off junction 3 of the M54. There are no less than 70 aircraft here, from the ill-fated TSR2, scrapped by Harold Wilson, to biplane-era aircraft; German planes and even the Mignet Flying Flea, which you built yourself! There are several exhibitions in addition and the entrance is free. Situated just over the county border in Shropshire, this attraction compliments Weston Park, Chillington Hall, Moseley Old Hall and Boscobel House (see below), all in reasonably close proximity to each other.

North of Weston Park is **Boscobel House**, now in the possession of English Heritage. It dates from 1632 and was initially a refuge for persecuted Roman Catholics, having a priest-hole in the attic. In 1651 it found another purpose. It was here that Charles II took sanctuary after losing the Battle of Worcester. He had escaped to Moseley Old Hall nearby and found his route to Wales blocked by Cromwell's troops. Hiding initially in an oak tree (the origin of the Royal Oak name of many English pubs) he spent a night in the priest-hole at Boscobel House.

The uncrowned king of England made his escape to France and founded the Grenadier Guards whilst in Bruges in 1656. The connection still remains, with every monarch since Charles II being a member of the Guild of St. Sebastian (an archers' guild) based in Bruges. He returned to England for his restoration in 1660.

Above left: RAF Museum Cosford; above right: Wightwick Manor (N.T.) west of Wolverhampton

Places to Visit

Boscobel House (E.H.)

Open: Easter–end-Oct, 10am-5pm daily (closed Mon & Tue), open at Bank Holiday Mondays.

Chillington House

Codsall Wood
Wolverhampton, WV8 1RE
☎ 01902 850236
www.chillingtonhall.co.uk
Open: Easter, May & Aug BH Sun & Mon. August (Wed-Fri & Sun). July - Sun. Grounds open every Sun Easter to end of May.

Halfpenny Green Vineyard & Craft Centre

Halfpenny Green
South Staffs, DY7 5EP
☎ 01384 221122
www.halfpenny-green-vineyards.co.uk
Open: Mon-Fri 10am-5pm; Sat-Sun 9.30-5pm
ⓟ ♿ 👫 (free) ☂

Holy Austin Rock Houses (N.T.)

Compton Road
Kinver
Stourbridge, DY7 6DL
☎ 01384 872553
Open: Sat-Sun 1ˢᵗ Mar–30ᵗʰ Nov, 2-4pm
Kinver Edge open all year
ⓟ 👫 ☂

RAF Museum Cosford

Shifnal
Shropshire, TF11 8UP
☎ 01902 376200
www.rafmuseum.org

Open daily 10-6pm (incl. BH), closed Christmas, New Year's Day (check for early Jan)
ⓟ ♿ 👫 (free, except airfield event days) ☂

Rodbaston Visitor Centre Animal Zone

Rodbaston College
Nr. Penkridge
☎ 01785 710560
www.rodbaston.ac.uk/visitorcentre
Wide variety of exotic, farm and companion animals.
A449 south from junction 13.
Open: Daily Mar–Oct, 10am-5pm, rest of year 10am-4pm (shop and tearoom). Animal zone only weekends and during school holidays.
ⓟ ♿ 👫 (farm ticket) No dogs except guide dogs.

Weston Park

Weston under Lizard
Shifnal
Shropshire, TF11 8LE
☎ 01952 852100
www.weston-park.com
Open: Easter–Aug weekends and BH, daily most of Jul & Aug.

Wightwick Manor (NT)

Wightwick Bank
Wolverhampton, WV6 8EE
☎ 01902 761400

Access

The county is crossed by the M5/M6, M54 and the M42 runs close to Burton on Trent.

Trains

Stoke on Trent, Stafford & Lichfield are on the London-Manchester line and the area is crossed by the Stoke-Derby route.

Airports

Major nearby airports are Birmingham, Nottingham, East Midlands and Manchester. Wolverhampton and Coventry also have airports.

Accommodation

This list is a compilation and not from the author's personal use. Local Tourist Information Centres offer a booking bureau and can advise on what is available to suit your requirements. As in most places, there is plenty to choose from.

Staying Somewhere Special

Hotels and Guest Houses

Weston Hall
Weston ST18 0BA
On Stafford - Uttoxeter Road, just off the A51
☎ 01889 271700
www.westonhall.co.uk

Hoar Cross Hall/Beauty Spa
Near Yoxall, Hoar Cross, Burton-on-Trent DE13 8QS
www.hoarcross.co.uk
High quality spa hotel, describes itself as one of the most prestigious in England. 4 Star.

Swan Hotel
46 Greengate Street, Stafford ST16 2JA
☎ 01785 258142
www.thelewispartnership.co.uk
18th Century hotel in pedestrianised town centre street, two doors from

largest timber framed town house in the country (Ancient High House Museum). The building itself is 17th century.

Izaak Walton Hotel
Ilam, Nr. Ashbourne,
Derbyshire DE6 2AY
☎ 017801335 350555
www.izaakwaltonhotel.com
Situated at the entrance to Dovedale. Has own fishing in River Dove in Dovedale (Staffordshire bank).

Colton House
Colton, Rugeley WS15 3LL
☎ 01889 578580
www.coltonhouse.com
Restored Georgian Grade II* listed guest house in 1.5 acre garden near Cannock Chase. 5 Star accommodation.

Self Catering

Alton Railway Station
Landmark Trust
Alton, Nr. Cheadle
Bookings: ☎ 01628 825925
www.landmarktrust.org.uk
Situated on disused line in lovely
Churnet Valley. Line is now a trail/cycle
route from Oakamoor - Denstone.
Sleeps 8. Italianate Station below Alton
Towers.

Blithfield Lakeside Barns
St. Stephens Hill Farm, Admaston,
Rugeley WS15 3NQ
☎ 01889 500234
www.blithfieldlakesidebarns.co.uk
At side of Blithfield Reservoir; all with
private patio and exceptionally high
standard. Near Abbots Bromley.

Church Farm
Stanshope, Nr. Alstonefield, DE6 2AD
☎ 01335 310243
www.dovedalecottages.co.uk
Two cottages and converted barn (5
Star). Sleeps 4 and 6.

Foxtwood Cottages
Foxt Road, Froghall ST10 2HJ
☎ 01538 266160
www.foxtwood.co.uk
Modern block of cottages on Caldon
Canal at Froghall Wharf. Great location.
Take your boots; try the Three Inns
Walk: Fox & Goose, Foxt/Marquis of
Granby, Ipstones/Black Lion, Consall
Forge. Paths for most of the way; canal
towpath, Consall Forge – Froghall or
steam train. Good food at all three inns.
All three open allday most of the year.

Guest Houses

Manor House Farm
Prestwood, Denstone ST14 5DD
☎ 01889 590415
www.4posteraccom.com
Jacobean farmhouse. Described as being 'a
haven for the discerning holidaymaker.'

Youth Hostels
There are three in north Staffordshire to a good quality.

YHA Alstonfield
Gypsy Lane, Alstonfield
Sleeps 20 but splits 8 and 12 if you wish
to hire rather than take a family room
for 4.

YHA Sheen Farm Bunkhouse
Sheen, Near Hartington
Near Church. Sleeps 14 in 2 rooms of 8
and 6 if you wish to hire.

YHA Ilam Hall
Ilam, Nr. Ashbourne
Major refurbishment winter 2008-9.
Family rooms available. Self catering
or meals available. A large YHA Centre
with bar.

All three in superb settings.
☎ For all three: YHA Contact Centre 0800
592 700.

Other Self Catering Booking Agencies

Peak District Farm Holidays
☎ 01629 540262
www.peakdistrictfarmhols.co.uk
For farmhouse B&B and self catering country cottages.
Also: www.staffordshireshortbreaks.co.uk

Stately Home Vacations

Charles Hurt's ancestors have lived at Casterne Hall, near Ilam, since the late 15th century. Now he offers exclusive accommodation and tours of Peak District country houses by the owner (or previous owner e.g. Lord Curzon at Kedleston Hall - now National Trust). Sir Richard Fitzherbert shows you around Tissington Hall, Lord Edward Manners around Haddon Hall and Charles at Casterne Hall etc. Stay and dine at both Tissington and Casterne. Tours also include an exclusive guided tour around Chatsworth (but not by the Duke of Devonshire!).

Short breaks of this exclusivity are not cheap, but if you want the ultimate in visiting somewhere special, contact Mark Chichester-Clark at Stately Home Vacations. The number of houses to visit and stay in is hopefully going to increase. ☎ 01335 310438. www.statelyhomevacations.com.

Discount Tickets

The Thrill Hopper ticket enables you as a single or as a family to entry to Alton Towers, Drayton Manor Theme Park, the Tamworth Snowdome and Water World, Stoke-on-Trent at a reduced rate. There are significant savings to be made by purchasing the Thrill Hopper ticket if you intend to visit more than one of these attractions in any one season. Go to www.thrillhopper.com to find out more.

Eating Out

The best advice on such a subjective matter as good food is to get a copy of the *Guide to Eating Out in Staffordshire*. It covers local dishes to international cuisine and is produced by the County Tourism Office. Call 0844 888 5205 or visit www. enjoystaffordshire.com for your copy.

Above: For Balloon flights see p.93   Below: Aerial Extreme, Trentham

Food & Beverage

Staffordshire has left its mark nationally where food is concerned: Marmite, Bovril & Branston Pickle all have their origins using bi-products of the brewing industry at Burton-on-Trent. Bird's Custard Powder is now made in the county, at Eccleshall and Knighton.

In North Staffordshire, other than the Oatcake (see separate feature), Wright's pies are an institution. The Company has its own shops and they are also widely distributed. Another local dish is 'lobby'. It basically consists of a stew made out of anything close to hand, especially the remains of a chicken (for instance) and cheap vegetables. It is very filling and costs little to produce. You are not likely to find it for sale, however!

Like most counties, Staffordshire has a range of small breweries. Titanic in Stoke-on-Trent is perhaps one of the best known, but others include Wincle of Rushton Spencer; Peakstones Rock of Alton; Slaters of Eccleshall; Enville; Kinver; with newcomer Lymestone at Stone.

Another small brewery is the Staffordshire Cheese Co and Leek Brewery, makers of bottle conditioned beers and also handmade cheeses. The latter includes The Staffordshire, a traditional clothbound cheese now with Protected Designation of Origin status. ☎ 01538 361919

Of course, Staffordshire is the home of Burton-on-Trent, still with its various breweries, including Marstons and Burton Bridge Breweries both producers of high quality cask beers.

In Derbyshire but only a field away from the Staffordshire border, at Hartington is the Stilton cheese factory with a factory shop in the village selling a range of cheeses. Hartington is also the home of Whim Ales, available in the Staffordshire Moorlands. Another speciality cheese is Innes goat's cheese from Tamworth.

Look out for local produce at the Farmers' Markets too, plus other local markets, such as the trestle market at the back of the Butter Market in Leek's Market Place, open Wednesdays and Saturdays.

Halfpenny Vineyard produces Staffordshire Wine near Wombourne and also sells a variety of locally produced products including aromatherapy oils, herbs and olives (see ch.7).

Farmers' Markets

Eccleshall, High Street	4th Saturday
Leek, Market Place	3rd Saturday (Festival of Fine Foods)
Stafford, Market Square	2nd Saturday
Stone, Market Square	1st Saturday
Tixall & Ingestre, Village Hall	1st Saturday
Newcastle	3rd Friday
Uttoxeter	Last Saturday in the month

Balloon Flights

Wickers World
☎ 01889 882222
www.wickersworld.co.uk
Flights from Shugborough Hall, Civil
Aviation Authority licensed.

Tourist Information Centres

Burton upon Trent
Horninglow Street, DE14 1NG
☎ 01283 508111
www.enjoyeaststaffs.co.uk

Cannock
Museum of Cannock Chase
Valley Road, Hednesford, WS12 5TD
☎ 01543 877666
www.cannockchasedc.gov.uk/museum

Leek
1 Market Place, ST13 5HH
☎ 01538 483741
www.staffsmoorlands.gov.uk

Lichfield
Lichfield Garrick, Castle Dyke,
WS13 6HR
☎ 01543 412112
www.visitlichfield.co.uk

Newcastle-under-Lyme
The Library, Ironmarket, ST5 1AT
☎ 01782 297313
www.newcastle-staffs.gov.uk

Stafford
Market Street, ST16 2LQ
☎ 01785 619619
www.visitstafford.org

Stoke-on-Trent
Victoria Hall, Bagnall Street, Hanley,
ST1 3AD
☎ 01782 236000
www.visitstoke.co.uk

Tamworth
29 Market Street, B79 7LR
☎ 01827 709581
www.visittamworth.co.uk

Well Dressing

Although well dressing in the county was recorded in 1680 (sic) by Dr. Robert Plot,
only a few villages celebrate the custom today. One is at Endon, near Leek. The event
is at the Spring Bank Holiday weekend. The other is Longnor, on the first Thursday
(Longnor Races) after the first Saturday in September.

Index

Index